Arthur von Studnitz

Gold

Or, legal regulations for the standard of gold and silver wares in different countries

of the world

Arthur von Studnitz

Gold

Or, legal regulations for the standard of gold and silver wares in different countries of the world

ISBN/EAN: 9783337427078

Printed in Europe, USA, Canada, Australia, Japan

Cover: Foto ©ninafisch / pixelio.de

More available books at **www.hansebooks.com**

GOLD:

OR,

LEGAL REGULATIONS FOR THE STANDARD OF GOLD & SILVER WARES IN DIFFERENT COUNTRIES OF THE WORLD.

TRANSLATED AND ABRIDGED FROM
"DIE GESETZLICHE REGELUNG DES FEINGEHALTES VON GOLD- UND SILBER-WAAREN, VON ARTHUR VON STUDNITZ,"

BY MRS. BREWER.

WITH NOTES AND ADDITIONS

By EDWIN W. STREETER.

London:
CHATTO & WINDUS, PICCADILLY.
1877.

PREFACE.

SHOULD the precious metals, which, in a definite purity, form the material of a nation's currency, receive any warranty or not, when used as an article of commerce?

The arguments against any guarantee of the genuineness of *precious metal ware* I lay before the reader in the following translation of Herr Studnitz, which is now presented for the first time to the English public.

The arguments in favour of such warranty I venture to sketch briefly in the following preface.

It is contended, then, that it can admit of no doubt whatever, that the governing institutions of a civilised country must be so framed as to protect the personal rights and the property of the members of the community. Whatever may be the amount of freedom granted to persons to trade, the liberty to do violence to the person, or to cheat, defraud, or injure the property of another, cannot be connived at by laws which regulate the intercourse of men; and experience has shown that, the higher the civilization, the more intricate and searching are the laws which are passed to protect from fraud.

It is incredible that any should be found to advocate the propriety of the sanction of the law being given to the utterance of a fraud. If the defenders of a fraud maintain that the liberty to cheat is beneficial to trade, let their statement stand alone; but let not the sanction of the law be claimed for the cheat.

Machiavelli did indeed instruct a ruler that any devices might be practised on his people for the object of government, and he deemed this sort of fraud only a natural development of the ethics of the most approved of heathen philosophers; but it remains for less scrupulous advocates still to extend this principle to the general dealings of citizens with each other, the law itself intervening to give currency to the swindle.

"Hall-marking," established to guarantee to the public the genuineness of precious metals, was instituted on the supposition that the assay and test of precious metals was a matter too recondite to render an adequate discrimination of so valuable a transfer of property a reasonable demand to be expected of the public generally. It could not be said that the transferee or purchaser, by the exercise of due caution, might protect his own interests sufficiently. It was not denied that the laws of the land might be appealed to in each case of fraud, and the courts would take all the facts into their consideration; but the legislature was not anxious to multiply litigation needlessly, and all governments have claimed an interest in the transfer of the precious metals which are the standard of the currency.

If the currency is a matter the purity of which greatly affects the stability of the country and the morality of the people, the material of the currency itself, as well as the name currently given to it, cannot be left to be manipulated for the sole advantage of a particular class of manufactures and trades. If gold be the name, and a particular and specified fineness of this gold the material, then it is pretty evident that, although the currency is rather the waggon which conveys than the material itself of a nation's wealth, yet the " waggon " must not be so fragile or so untrustworthy as to render its use uncertain and dangerous.

Why should the people be deprived of the security which the government deems so essential to its own protection? While the whole of the circumstances essential to the protection of the community in the formation of new schemes of investment are regulated by law, why should the very material itself—the very name "gold"—which represents the value of the shares—be left to the devices of any fraudulent trader who chooses to impose on his unscientific customer for his individual benefit, without any regard to the ultimate injury devolved on "society"?

If, however, it be deemed advisable to carry the doctrines of "free trade" to the extent of licensing every man to outvie his neighbour in the coinage of deception, let not the sanction of the law be practically given to this deception. If brass, and iron, and plaster of Paris may be sold for gold, at least let not the "*stamping and Hall-marking*" be pledged in substantiation of the fraud. If a great guild, bearing an ancient charter, vouches for the fulfilment of the conditions of this guarantee, let the gold be of a fineness to be easily ascertained by the purchaser and transferee. Coffee may not be sold as coffee when mixed with any other grain, however beneficial, but must, on pain of penalty, be called by some other name and sold as a mixture. Even so let "gold" (a name bearing a special signification) be hedged about at least sufficiently to prevent the most annoying and injurious frauds, which are rendering the trade in precious metal wares abroad anything but savoury.

That certain artists in metallic work are deprived of employment because they cannot sell iron and copper, lead and brass, and tin and zinc for gold, is an argument which is very gravely urged. If the work commends the artist, the sale is a most legitimate and laudable one; but if only the fraud commends the artist, why should the argument have weight?

Fraud is not needful to bolster up free trade. By all means let every encouragement be given to art as such, but it is the death-blow of art to substitute the false for the true.

If the object of legislation is to pit cunning against cunning, and drive the weakest in this contest to the wall, we must as a nation profess the "*Rogues' Creed.*"

If the man who coins a base sovereign is a

criminal in the eye of the law, why should not the trader who marks his spurious gold with a stamp intended to deceive his customer for Hall-marking be also so deemed?

Gold marked by the Hall should be of a recognised value. It should be the 18-carat, or higher, if those values be now sufficiently recognised. If any tradesman desires to sell works of art which he deems to have a higher value than the material of which they are made, let him mark them with his own name, state the *value* of the composite matter (the carat value), and trust to his genius for the sale, and not to the falsehood of a cunning imitation of the Hall-mark.

Let these rules be known and universally adopted, and then the man who purchases may fairly be expected to use the needful caution to afford him adequate protection. Trade generally would be less liable to ultimate loss from fraudulent appearances, and competition would be absolutely freed from injurious conditions, and fine art in metal work might be expected to revive.

It is well known that I have myself, at all risk to my trade, persevered in offering only the 18-carat gold. Whatever machinery could do and skill could accomplish to render my articles moderate in price and acceptable as works of art and of ascertained value, I have done persistently. The gold thus transferred is of its marked current value, no matter how long it may have been used in the shape of articles of ornament or luxury. It may be said that I have no reason to complain of the result, but others with less stock-in-trade and less means of display have not the same chances; and, while I admit that the repute and protection of trade generally have much influenced my crusade against " fraudulent gold " ware, I maintain that the confidence of the public, derived from a reassurance of the genuine character of our jewellery trade, is worth all the temporary sacrifice which this safer path is likely to entail.

EDWIN W. STREETER.

CONTENTS.

	PAGE
PART I.—Introduction	15
PART II.—The Laws of all Countries of the World concerning the Standard of Gold and Silver Wares	25
Great Britain	25
British Colonies	35
France	35
Denmark	49
Turkey	50
Greece	51
Belgium	51
Holland	55
Italy	56
Spain	60
Portugal	60
Austria	61
Russia	66
Switzerland. Cantons:— Basle. Zurich. Soleure. Glarus. Lucerne. Pays de Vaud. Neufchatel. Geneva. Remaining Cantons.	68
Sweden	71
Norway	72
Prussia	72
Bavaria	72
Saxony	72
Hesse	72
Mecklenburgh-Strelitz	73

Oldenburgh	73
Brunswick	73
Hamburg	73
Bremen	74
Lübeck	74
Other European Towns	74
America	74
Egypt	74
Morocco	75
China	75
Persia	75
PART III.	80
PART IV.	85
PART V.	86
PART VI.	100
PART VII.	125

PART I.

INTRODUCTION.

STANDARD is the term used to express the relation between the pure gold and silver in precious metal goods and coins, and the alloy with which it is mixed. The degrees of standard were formerly expressed, in the case of gold, by carats (the dried kernel of the locust-bean), of which, in Germany, twenty-four were called a mark. The carat was further divided into twelve grains. Twenty-four-carat gold was of absolute purity.

In England this manner of determining the standard quality of gold is still in use.

The standard of alloyed silver was formerly indicated everywhere by its weight; and it still is so indicated in many countries.

Sixteen-ounce silver is *pure* silver.

An ounce divides itself into eighteen "*grains.*"

Following the example of France, it is now usual to indicate the standard of silver and gold by $\frac{1}{10.0}$ parts.

As a rule, there are three methods of deciding the standard, the oldest being *the stripe test*.

In the goldsmiths' regulations at Ulm, in the year 1394, we find the following :—" In testing gold, a *stripe stone* shall be made use of, *according to old custom*."

This is, in fact, an old custom; for the Ancient Greeks made use of such a stone, which was called Βάυαυορ, from the purpose for which it was employed; and sometimes of *Lydian stone*, so termed because it was found in the river Imolus in Lydia.

This testing-stone is black, and consists of black jasper or stone of Lydia; and the quality of the silver is judged of according to the colour of the stripe which it leaves upon the testing-stone when drawn across it.

To insure a correct decision, the stripe of the article which is being tested is compared with the stripe made in the same manner by the *testing needles*, as they are called, which are of various known standards, and of which each tester possesses a great number. In the stripe test as applied to gold, the standard is determined by the manner in which the nitric acid, freed from the oxymuriatic acid, acts upon the stripe of the alloy being tested.

The *stripe test*, however, serves only for a superficial decision of the standard. It is especially deceptive when the silver contains large quantities of zinc or nickel, because these metals used as alloy alter the colour but little.

In later times gold has frequently been alloyed with zinc; especially in America has this been done. This alloy has a very beautiful colour, but proportionately the standard is reduced to the lowest degree. Thus it happens that in melting old silver articles an alloy of zinc is often found, this metal having been included in the standard of such articles.

A more exact method is the *test by fire*.

Here a small quantity of the silver to be tested (a definite weight) is refined in a small crucible made of beech-wood ash and bone-dust, or else of bone-dust alone, saturated with vegetable salts. The silver is mixed with lead and melted under a cover. By this means the inferior metal is oxydized and absorbed in a molten condition by the porous substance of the cup, while the pure silver remains behind in the form of a small flattened bead or corn.

The weight of this bead, compared with the weight of alloyed metal which was originally employed in the process, shows the standard of the silver.

It is important that the refining process should be carried on with the least possible amount of heat, to prevent the too rapid evaporization of the lead. There is a proverb among the workmen which runs thus :—

"Kühle getrieben und heisser Blick,
Ist der Probirkunst Meisterstück."

In the latter part of the reign of Charles X. of France, Gay-Lussac introduced a new method of testing silver, as he himself modestly admits in the preface to his work, entitled, "Complete instructions as to the proceeding of testing silver in the *wet way*" (a work which was translated by Liebig, and published in the year 1833).

Tillet had already made known, in the memoirs of the Royal Academy of Science, between the years 1761 and 1769, that the process of refining silver from its alloy yielded by some thousandths too little.

Tillet's experiments, however, were soon forgotten, or rather it was somewhat hazardous

INTRODUCTION.

to attack a process upon which all commerce in silver was grounded, and which was in common use almost everywhere. Moreover, the necessity of a change for the better was the less felt, inasmuch as no complaints were raised about it, and because the loss occasioned by the under-estimation of the value of the silver goods passed unnoticed from the seller to the buyer.

Thus it was that the practice was transmitted from one age to another, and was closely adhered to by those who were successively employed in carrying it out in the Mint, and in the Stamp and Control Offices. In the meantime, while the advances made in the art of refining proved the possibility of extracting profit even to the $\frac{1}{1000}$ part of gold from silver, a large quantity of pure silver accumulated daily in the Mints.

Now, since pure silver deteriorated in the crucible only to the extent of $\frac{1}{1000}$ or $\frac{2}{1000}$, and alloyed silver of $\frac{900}{1000}$ standard lost $\frac{4}{1000}$ or $\frac{5}{1000}$ in value, it followed, as a necessary consequence, that a director of the Mint receiving pure silver to be coined into pieces of money of $\frac{900}{1000}$ standard was compelled to make the actual standard of such pieces of money $\frac{993}{1000}$ or $\frac{994}{1000}$, that they might answer to $\frac{999}{1000}$ when tested in the laboratory of the Commissioners of the Mint. The director began, therefore, to sustain in such coinage a loss of from $\frac{3}{1000}$ to $\frac{4}{1000}$; and the cause of this could not long remain concealed from him. In this way arose the complaints which led to a fresh investigation of the testing process as carried on with the crucible.

The new test, called the *Titrir Method*, or *Wet Test*, demands a previous approximate decision of the standard by means of the *stripe* or *fire tests*, and admits itself of the greatest precision. It is carried out in this manner:

Either a definite weight of alloyed silver is dissolved in nitric acid, and the silver in solution precipitated as chloride of silver by means of a solution of common salt, in which case the standard of the alloy is reckoned by the quantity of solution of common salt required for this purpose; or else from gold is produced oxyd of gold, free from oxyd of iron; the oxyd of gold made soluble in oxymuriatic acid, and amalgamated with oxalic acid; and the amount of oxalic acid which does not become oxydized, determined.

Under the head of *Gold Tests* is included the following :—

"In the case of silver being contained *in* gold, the relative value of the silver and gold is decided by driving off the gold in the crucible. In deciding the standard of gold alone, however, it is melted at once in the crucible with a corresponding quantity of silver and lead, and the finally remaining bead of silver which contains the gold is afterwards treated with nitric acid." (*Millaner.*)

These, however, are only the most usual methods of deciding the intrinsic standard. Of several which are interesting in the same department of science, we would particularise only one, namely, that of Archimedes, whose exultant "Eureka" signified, not that he had simply found out the way to determine the standard of the crown of King Iliero, but especially that he had enriched the world with a fundamental hydrostatic law—a discovery in the strictest sense of the word.

How far the art of working in gold and silver had been cultivated among the ancients, and how well they understood mixing the precious metals with alloy, is best seen in Livy's

"Roman History" (I., xxxii., c. 2), where it is mentioned that the quæstors showed the silver paid by the Carthaginians as tribute to be *impure*, and on the application of the fire test it was found to be deficient in value by ¼.

Even in the time of the prophet Malachi we read (c. iii. v. 2, 3)—"For he is like a refiner's fire . . . He shall sit as a refiner and purifier of silver, and he shall purify . . . and purge them as gold and silver."

Nowhere do we meet with any intimation that the State undertook the supervision of the manufacture of precious metal wares, either for the purpose of drawing financial profit from such a supervision, or in order to protect the purchasing public.

The fact that the necessity for State control of this kind was nowhere manifested has the greater claim to attention, because at that time chemical and physical knowledge was by no means so widely spread as now, and because there were fewer people from whom information could be derived as to the value of objects in gold and silver.

Summing up the question of standards in the Roman law, Mr. Charles Roscher, in his work upon the "Legal Regulations of the Manufactures of Gold and Silver," calls attention to the following :—" Whoever bought brass for gold, or lead or any other silvery-looking body for silver; whoever bought a table plated with silver for massive silver, might, according to the Pandects, regard the purchase as void, because he had not received that for which he stipulated. Whoever, on the contrary, bought alloyed gold, which he erroneously considered to be of higher standard than it was, was compelled, if he bought the object merely as '*gold*,' without any condition of a definite standard, to consider the bargain valid against himself."

This principle applied even to the case of a person purchasing at a high price an old bracelet, which in all its parts was valued as gold, whereas the greater part of it subsequently proved to be *copper*, and only a little gold mixed with it. "For," says Ulpian, "it did truly contain gold."

"This is in strict accordance," writes Puebla, "with the principle that the character of a bargain does not depend upon the just proportion of the price paid. On the contrary, the demand for such a just proportion would disturb commerce." A maxim which in Roman law was expressly intended to provide that no unfair opposition should be offered to trade.

The development of the Guilds, having for their apparent object the protection of the public, but in reality intended to prevent competition, led at first to restrictions on the working of precious metals. The oldest regulation of the kind in England seems to have been issued in the year 1238.

Since, as will be seen later, the legal regulation of the standard of precious metal wares has, in all States, been subject to very frequent changes, and since it may be safely predicted that further changes will occur in most of them, we judged that it would be useful to add to this work a collection, as comprehensive as possible, of all the old stipulations and laws relating to the regulation of the standard of gold and silver ware. We applied, therefore, to every government, not only for information as to the various laws and regulations at present in force, but also for brief reports of the discussions which preceded the several legal changes effected by the various representative assemblies.

PART II.

THE LAWS OF ALL COUNTRIES OF THE WORLD CONCERNING THE STANDARD OF GOLD AND SILVER WARES.

GREAT BRITAIN.

IT is more than six centuries since the first decrees concerning the legal regulation of the standard of gold and silver wares were made in England. These date from the year 1238, in the reign of Henry III.; when, in consequence of fraud, it apparently was necessary to direct the gold and silversmiths that no one should manufacture gold of less value than one hundred shillings per mark, or silver of a lower standard than that of the silver coinage.

The transfer to the London Goldsmiths' Company of the privilege (which holds good to the present day) of testing ware made of the precious metals took place in the year 1300, in the reign of Edward I.

This act forbade the manufacture of any

gold ware of lower standard than that of Paris; and by it the silver ware was required to be, at the lowest, of the standard of the silver coinage, and to be stamped with a leopard's head. Before any piece of work in the precious metals left the workshop, it had to be tested by the inspector specially appointed for the purpose. All wares in the precious metals which were not so rich as the legally fixed standard, were to be forfeited to the king; the offenders being *threatened* with punishment or fine at the king's pleasure.

These regulations at first only applied to London, but they were afterwards extended to the provinces.

In the year 1327, the first of Edward III.'s reign, the Goldsmiths' Company was charged to punish those who so cleverly overlaid tin with silver that their goods were taken for, and sold as, fine silver.

An ordinance of the Goldsmiths' Company in the year 1336 revoked the provisions of the law of the year 1300, and appointed that the manufacturer shall stamp his wares of precious metals. A law of 1363 confirmed the last part of this ordinance.

A law passed in the year 1379 (Richard II.) adds to the stamp of the manufacturer that of the town or district in which the work shall have been stamped, and also that of the king.

A law passed in 1392, in the same reign, conferred fresh authority on the Goldsmiths' Company.

In 1403 (Henry IV.) it was enacted that no copper or brass work, except church ornaments, shall be gilt or silvered, and even these must be left unplated in one part, so that the metal of which they consisted might be recognised.

An ordinance of the year 1405 decided a dispute between the crafts of the Goldsmiths and Cutlers, settling that the latter had the right to work in gold and silver, but that their work must be tested by the craft of Goldsmiths.

In 1414 (Henry V.) silver work was forbidden to be gilt, if it did not come up at least to the standard of the silver coinage; while an enactment of 1420 forbade the silvering of any metal, excepting the spurs of a knight, the accoutrements of a baron or of one of a higher rank, or church ornaments.

In 1423 (Henry VI.) it was repeated that no

precious metal wares should be offered for sale which did not bear the stamp of the guild and of the manufacturer.

In 1462 (Edward IV.) the right of the London Goldsmiths' Company was extended to the testing of precious metal wares in Chester, Newcastle, Norwich, Exeter, Birmingham, and Sheffield.

A statute passed in 1477 (Edward IV.), reciting that the law made by Henry VI. was daily evaded, fixed the standard of gold ware at 18 carats; that of silver ware continuing, as before, uniform with that of the silver coinage. This law was re-inforced in 1489 and 1552.

By a law passed in 1488 (Henry VII.), in which it is declared that the refiners of gold and silver do not observe the regulations affecting the standard of precious metal wares, and that they buy gilt silver from the Mint, the Exchange, and the goldsmiths, which they mix with alloy as they please, insomuch that no pure silver is to be obtained when required, to the great damage of the king's nobles and the Commons, the alloying of gold and silver and the sale of all alloyed metal were restricted to the officers of the Mint and Exchange.

GOLD.

In 1504 it was legally reaffirmed that the laws respecting the standard of precious metal wares were often evaded, and in 1573 (Elizabeth) it was enjoined that gold ware should thenceforth have a standard of at least 22 carats, and silver ware a standard of 11 ounces 2 dwts.

It is interesting to note how in this enactment, as in several others, the good old times are looked back upon in which better gold and silver were manufactured; and yet it is evident that, had this really been the case, the rulers would not have found it necessary to make such a series of laws with regard to these objects; each one treading upon the heels of another, and all, in spite of their number, incompetent to deal satisfactorily with transgressions of the law.

In 1576 (Elizabeth) the determinations of the enactment of 1573 were legally fixed.

In the books of the London Goldsmiths' Company of the year 1597, a report is made upon the frauds and counterfeit stamps of two goldsmiths who were sentenced to be placed in the pillory at Westminster, with their ears nailed to it, and tickets over their heads upon which their offences were written. From Westminster they were brought to the pillory at

Cheapside, where each offender had an ear cut off; after which they were conducted through Foster Lane to the Fleet Prison. In addition to all this disgrace and suffering, they had to pay a fine of ten marks. This was the usual punishment in most countries for similar offences.

In Belgium, goldsmiths who manufactured precious metals of a lower standard than that allowed by law, were taken to the market-place of their town, and there nailed by the ears to a pillory, being compelled to remain in that position till they had purchased their freedom by the surrender of a portion of their ears.

An order of the London Goldsmiths' Company in the year 1695, reciting that the laws relating to the standard are often evaded, inculcates them anew.

A law of the year 1697 (William III.) promises to all who shall within a given time bring manufactured silver to one of the royal mints, a fixed price per ounce. This was occasioned by the alteration of the legal standard of silver ware.

In the same year the standard of silver ware was raised to 11 ounces 10 dwts., and the figure of the stamp to be used by the manufacturer and by the London Goldsmiths' Guild was settled.

In 1698 (William III.) the export of manufactured silver was forbidden. Mr. William Chaffers * is of opinion that this measure was at that time a good and beneficial one, because it had the tendency to keep at home the metal of the coinage, to the welfare of the kingdom. This law, however, was in force only a very short time, as manufactured silver was again permitted to be exported under certain conditions.

The laws of 1700 (William III.), and of 1702 (Anne), order the establishment of Control Offices at York, Exeter, Chester, Norwich, and Newcastle-upon-Tyne, the testers of the London Goldsmiths' Guild, in consequence of the alteration of the legal standard of silver ware, being over-occupied, and the necessity of sending their goods to London to be stamped being attended with great inconvenience to the goldsmiths of these towns.

A law of the year 1719 (George I.), recording that silver ware manufactured according to the standard earlier in use was more durable than

* "Hall Marks on Gold and Silver Plate."

that manufactured after the new standard, decrees that no goldsmith is *compelled* to work at the standard of 11 ounces 10 dwts., but permits the use of this standard, and also of that of 11 ounces 2 dwts. The same law imposes a duty of sixpence per ounce upon imported silver and silver manufactured abroad.

In 1739 (George II.) the precious metals used by jewellers were exempted from the necessity of bearing a fixed standard. Other directions were also laid down as to the stamps to be applied. This law adverts to the prevalence of fraud.

In 1756 (George II.) the import duty upon manufactured silver was lowered to sixpence upon 10 ounces.

In 1758 the punishment for counterfeit stamping was increased to the term of fourteen years' transportation.

In 1759 (George II.) the dues to be paid by the goldsmiths to the king for their license were increased.

In 1797 the duty upon gold ware was fixed at 8*s.* per ounce, and upon silver at 1*s.* per ounce.

In 1798 (George III.) was legalised the manufacture of gold ware at 18 carats.

In 1803 new licensing duties were fixed for the manufacturers of precious metal ware; and in the subsequent year the duty on gold ware was raised to 16s. per oz., and that on silver ware to 1s. 3d. per oz.

In 1815 was enacted the most important of the rules now in force as to the duty upon precious metal wares; and in 1844 (Victoria) the penalties attached to counterfeit stamping of gold and silver ware were fixed.

The most recent English law upon the standard of gold and silver ware dates from the year 1854.

All gold and silver ware manufactured in the United Kingdom is required to be tested and stamped; the cost of stamping amounting to 17s. per oz. for gold ware, and 1s. 6d. per oz. for silver; and the duty is payable at the place of testing.

At the present time five legal standards exist for gold ware :—

    22 carat gold.
    18 ,, ,,
    15 ,, ,,
    12 ,, ,,
    9 ,, ,,

For silver ware there are two—11 oz. 10 dwt. and 11 oz. 2 dwts.

The lowering of the standard of precious metal ware met a great emergency.

Although English watches have always been in great demand in the United States of America, yet, owing to the quality of the standard, they were too costly. English watches *without* cases were therefore exported there. The Americans enclosed the watches in cases having a standard of from 10 to 16 carats, and sold them in South America and other markets at a price with which the English could not compete.

The following gold wares are exempt from the dues of stamping:—

Watch cases, gold setting for precious stones, chains, rings, buttons, bells, clasps for garters, necklaces, sliding pencils, needle cases, &c.

Among silver ware there is an exemption of watch cases, chains, beads, bracelets, necklaces, brooches, buckles, lockets, &c., of whatever weight these may be.

Many articles are also exempt which weigh less than 10 dwts.

The penalty incurred by those who sell or

export unstamped goods is £50, and, in case of inability to pay, confinement in a house of correction for periods varying from six months to a year.

The value of goods seized belongs half to the Crown and half to the informer. For exported goods of gold and silver an export premium is granted which amounts to the costs of stamping; for gold 17s. per oz., and for silver 1s. 6d.

In the British colonies no laws are in force which regulate the standard of gold and silver ware.

FRANCE.

The Minister of Finance in France has had the goodness to communicate to us that, in consequence of the disturbance of the archives, he is not in a position to forward to us the early laws regulating the standard of gold and silver wares. We therefore avail ourselves of the information supplied in the well-known work by William Chaffers upon the old French laws regulating the standard of gold and silver ware.

In the "Livre des Métiers," compiled by

Etienne Boileau, Provost of Paris, from 1258-1269, we find in the preface that "no goldsmith may work gold in Paris which is not of the Paris touch, or better; which touch or standard surpasses all the gold which is worked in any other country; and no silver must be worked which is not as good as, or better than, the sterling silver of England."

In an ordinance of Philippe le Hardi, 1275, the silver-workers were compelled to stamp their works with the sign of the town; and in the reign of Phillipe le Bel, 1313, gold was ordered to be stamped with the punch of the Goldsmiths' Company of Paris; and it was further ordered that each city should have a particular mark for works in silver.

The same king (Phillipe le Bel) decreed that the manufacture of gold and silver should be restricted to pieces of a certain weight. This was for the double purpose of limiting the progress of luxury, and of reserving a sufficient quantity of the precious metals for coinage.

Louis XI. and Louis XII. confirmed this decree; but as the Paris goldsmiths complained bitterly of this restriction, in consequence of the prelates, princes, and nobles getting their work done out of France, the king was induced to alter the law four years after, viz., in 1510.

An edict of the year 1554 commanded all goldsmiths, under fine of 1,000 livres and bodily punishment, to enter with their own hand in a register the weight of every piece of precious metal or precious metal ware, as well as the name of buyer or seller. This was somewhat modified in 1555; but it still exists in a milder form.

In 1631 a duty of *three sols* per ounce was laid upon all the precious metal work.

In 1633 this duty was compounded for by a sum of 24,000 livres, which the Paris goldsmiths had to pay, and 8,000 livres, which the wire-drawers and gold-beaters had to pay.

In 1672 the duty was re-established; and in 1674 it was still further increased.

In 1681 works of silver gilt were subjected to a like duty with silver. In this same year a fine of 3,000 livres, besides personal degradation, was inflicted for fixing the stamp of a high standard on false metal.

But for the same offence in the year 1724 the sentence was " d'être pendus et étranglés."

Although Louis XIV. had stood pre-eminent in his use, nay, in the extravagant display, of precious metal ware, yet when a time of great scarcity arrived, he sent about 10,000,000 francs' worth to the mint for the purpose of raising money, and made it compulsory that the nobility and gentry should do the same.

In March, 1700, the early edicts of Louis XIV. against the luxury of precious metal wares were made more stringent. Under penalty of 3,000 livres, and confiscation, no gold article was to weigh more than an ounce, and no silver ware above the weight of 8 marks. No one dared ornament their dress with gold or silver lace, nor were they allowed to use gold and silver to ornament carriage harness, liveries, or furniture of any kind. The result of these strict laws was that great quantities of gold and silver ware were imported, whilst the weight of the article to be manufactured was limited in 1721 to 7 ounces. At the same time the standard of small gold ware was fixed at $20\frac{1}{4}$ carats.

A law of 1746 decreed that the inner part, or under surface, of real gold lace should be of silk, and that of the false gold lace of red cotton; so that the two kinds of lace might be easily distinguished.

In 1763 a universal method of testing was commanded.

In 1765 the law determining that silver boxes lined with gold should be stamped with the word silver was remitted.

In 1769 it was required that all imported gold and silver ware should be tested and stamped in the " Maison Commune."

A law of 1782 instituted the use of a new punch.

In 1783 the standard of silver ware was fixed at 11 oz. 12 grains, and of gold ware at 20½ carats.

A law of 15th December, in the same year, gave to each of the Communes in France a separate stamp.

Concerning the legal regulations of the standard of gold and silver ware now in force in France, we have received the following information from Mons. de Parieu, who accompanies his communication with the remark " That the manufacture and the trade of gold and silver ware in France are placed under very strict regulations, which appear no longer in harmony with social progress and the principles of political science."

These regulations or restrictions are found in the laws of 19 Brumaire (November), 1797, and contain the following standards :—

$\frac{920}{1000}$ ...	$\frac{840}{1000}$ ...	$\frac{750}{1000}$ ...	for gold.
$\frac{950}{1000}$ ...	$\frac{800}{1000}$ ...	...	for silver.

The law of the 19th Brumaire, which is in force to the present day, declares in

Article 5.—That the allowance of alloy in gold is limited to $\frac{3}{1000}$, and in silver to $\frac{5}{1000}$.

Article 8.—All precious metal ware shall receive three distinct stamps; that of the manufacturer, that of the standard, and that of the Control Bureau. And, beyond these, stamps for imported and plated ware.

Article 21.—That the stamp duty per hectogramme for gold ware be 20 francs, and for silver ware 1 franc; to which is added the cost of testing.

Article 23.—Precious metal ware imported from foreign lands must be shown to the Custom House officers on the borders, who forward them to the next Control Bureau, where they are dealt with as the native produce. Exceptions to this rule are articles belonging to ambassadors, and which serve for the use of

GOLD. 41

travellers; but in the latter case the weight must not exceed 5 hectogrammes.

Article 25.—For French gold and silver ware exported an export duty must be paid amounting to ⅔ of the stamp duty.

Article 47.—Every officer, under pain of dismissal, is forbidden to give any description, either by word or in writing, of the precious metal articles in the Bureau.

Article 62.—The duty for testing the standard of gold ware is 3 francs each article, and for silver ware 80 rappes (a rappe ⅘ of a penny) each article.

Article 64.—For testing small gold ware with the testing stone, 9 rappes per deckagramme.

Article 65.—If the testing officer suspects that the precious metal ware contains within it copper, iron, or other matter, he may, in the presence of the owner, cut it. In case of his suspicion being confirmed, the owner is fined twenty times the value of the article, which is also confiscated, and he is given over to justice. If, on the other hand, he is wronged by the supposition, the injury to the article is made good.

Article 72.—The precious metal manufacturer is bound to deposit his stamp with the proper authorities.

Article 74.—The precious metal manufacturer and tradesmen are bound to inform one of the officers in charge of the register of the weight, the number, the standard, and the kind of goods bought or sold.

Article 75.—Manufacturers and tradesmen are only allowed to purchase gold and silver of such people as are known to them, or for whom they will be responsible.

Article 78.—The same are bound to hang up in their sale-rooms the laws connected with the sale and standard of precious metal ware.

Article 79.—The tradesman in gold and silver ware must provide the buyer with the date of his purchase and the place of purchase, the quality or standard, and weight of the article, and also whether it be new or old. Regular forms are obtainable at the Régie de l'Enregistrement.

Article 80.—Anyone transgressing any part of the articles, commencing with 72, will for the first offence be fined 200 francs; for the second, 300 francs; and for the third, 1,000 francs; and will be deprived of the privilege of carrying on any further business.

Article 81.—Whosoever shall sell precious metal ware with a false statement of standard renders himself liable to a fine of 200 francs for the first offence, 400 for the second, and 1,000 for the third, and is disqualified for the conduct of trade.

Article 86.—The manufacturer or tradesman of articles set in gold and silver is not bound to give such articles to the Control Bureau; but he is bound to keep a register in which all matters connected with the article purchased are to be entered.

Article 87.—As in the case of manufacturers and sellers of precious metal ware, so these are compelled to hand to the buyer a filled-up form concerning the purchased article.

Article 92.—The sellers of knives, &c., made of precious metal are bound to inform the proper authorities of what gold-workers the articles in which they trade have been purchased.

Article 95.—The manufacturer of plated precious metal ware is bound to give notice of it to the proper authorities and to the Mint.

Article 109.—Articles bearing a false stamp will be confiscated. Those who knowingly possess or sell articles with false stamps will be fined for the first offence 200 francs; for the second, 400 francs; and for the third, 1,000 francs; and will be debarred from further trade.

The law contained in Article 74 was made still more strict by a decree of the year 1821.

The great variety of stamps to which, in the course of time, French precious metals had been subjected, caused much perplexity to the officers of assize. To meet this complication an ingenious means of information was found, viz., *to provide all precious metal ware with a new stamp, the recense.* This was to be a stamp of verification for all the works of gold and silver then existing, and, as a rule, to be free of cost.

In 1836 the stamp or punch of the standard, and that of the Test or Assay Office, was to consist of one single stamp, which should bear a particular sign for each office (in 1838).

At the same time the *poinçon de remarque* was instituted—a stamp to be placed at every four inches on chains, or precious metal ware of that character. They are now marked every decimetre (a law of 1838).

It is very certain that these strict laws have failed in the object they had in view, viz., the suppression of deceit, as was lately acknowledged in the assembly; nor has the precious metal industry been improved by them.

In the interior of France one scarcely knows how sensibly the interests of the industries and the public are injured by the above restrictions, because the French public have never enjoyed the advantage of buying cheap precious metal ware, and the French manufacturers have never experienced how much the demand for their manufactures would increase if the law allowed them to manufacture at a low standard and price, and trust to the increase of trade for their profits. In foreign lands this is otherwise.

The French gold-workers see what a tremendous part the German and Geneva manufacturers play in the world; they must daily remark how their wares are the source of great gain to strangers, while they themselves cannot partake of it. It is true French metal wares are brought from abroad, but only in very small numbers, and often solely for the purpose of serving as *models*. The Paris commissioner selects the newest and most elegant article, buys a small number, and sends them either to Germany or Switzerland, where they are imitated by the hundred in a lower degree of standard. If the French manufacturer tries to bring his own ware to the world's market, he has to battle with the creation of his own taste and his own genius without ever being victorious, because the laws of his own land forbid the manufacture of cheap ware.

The French industry will not always be content with this. "La France réclame vigoureusement la liberté du titre pour faire une guerre industrielle à Allemagne," wrote a much respected Geneva gold-worker in March, 1873. Indeed, M. Tirard brought forward in the National Assembly a proposal to allow the gold-workers of France to work definite gold and silver ware for export according to what standard they please. The manufacturer, however, was to be compelled to stamp his name and the degree of standard on each of his finished works. For non-compliance with this requisition he was to be subject to a money fine, and to have his goods confiscated.

GOLD.

The debate which ensued on the introduction of this motion gave us an interesting insight into the condition of the French gold-worker. It showed that the stamp duty which burdened this industry had been lately increased 50 per cent., the gain to the Treasury thereby being 6,000,000 francs.

The chief centres of precious metal ware industry are Paris, Besançon, Lyons, and Marseilles.

Lyons pays yearly 100,000 francs stamp duty, and works principally for home consumption. At the same time it exports large quantities of goods which do not come under State control, such as are stitched or woven in with gold and silver. It is quite evident that in France the chief object of State control of the precious metal industries is not the protection of the public, but the enriching of the treasury.

Besançon pays from 800,000 to 1,000,000 francs stamp duty, generally upon watches; which shows us to what an extent this industry has grown here. Many more hands could be employed, if it were not that they are compelled, in consequence of the restrictions of the French laws, to send so large a number of their unfinished watches (most of them for re-exportation) to Geneva, where the gold may be of lower standard than is allowed in France.

M. Tirard, who brought forward this motion, called attention to the fact that no less than 140 Articles, incorporating laws and restrictions for the precious metal ware industries, were still in force, and were no less unfavourable to them now than eighty years ago; and that, owing to these laws, the English, Swiss, Dutch, and Germans exported French wares to the exclusion of the French themselves. Abroad there are but few French traders in the precious metal wares. The French nation are no traders; and those who engage in trade, deal not in French metal ware, but in German, and that to the amount of 30,000,000 francs annually. M. Tirard related that he himself tried in New York, and also in Mexico, to find French ware, hoping that where French troops had been, French taste would have spread; but he everywhere came across German manufactures.

The eloquent defender of the forementioned motion, which would have been so advantageous to the precious metal industries of France, was unable to carry it. It was rejected.

DENMARK.

We learn upon good authority (that of the Danish Finance Minister, through the Royal Mint and State Warden, Mr. S. Gross) that on the 7th of November, 1685, the king ordained that no silver should be worked of less standard than $13\frac{1}{2}$ lothig ($\frac{1}{2}$ oz.), remedium $\frac{1}{4}$ loth.; and that all the ware should, according to law, be marked with the stamp of the manufacturer, and then taken to the warden, who, if he found it correct, should stamp it with the Copenhagen arms (three towers) and his own initials.

Silver ware of higher standard was required to be marked with the higher standard stamp; and by a rescript of 15th June, 1770, a fine of from 3 to 150 shillings was imposed in respect of such ware as, upon completion, should fail two, three, or four grains in its standard. A circular of 16th June, 1792, made this still more stringent; silver-workers in the provinces being informed that, under pain of punishment, they were themselves to stamp the standard on each piece of their finished work.

As it happened in many other lands, the old laws had either lost their virtue or died out in Denmark. Gold ware, according to royal decision of 7th November, 1685, was to be either of 23 or 21 carats, and to be stamped with the letter *D* (ducat gold), or *C* (crown gold).

A royal rescript of 26th August, 1778, authorised the working of gold ware of 20 and 18 carats; and one of February 7, 1781, exempted small gold ware from stamping, and made the degree of standard for all gold ware optional, provided the goldsmith stamped each article with his name and the number of carats, for the accuracy of which he was answerable.

Precious metal ingots were to be stamped with either the standard or the city arms, and the initials of the warden.

TURKEY.

In Turkey there is no law by which the standard of gold ware is regulated.

Most of the gold ware here is of 22 carat, or $\frac{916\frac{2}{3}}{1000}$.

GOLD: 51

Previous to the year 1844, silver ware was required to have a minimum standard of $\frac{800}{1000}$; and since that time of $\frac{900}{1000}$.

Silver ware is stamped in the royal mint with the city stamp.

GREECE.

No law is in force to regulate the standard of precious metal ware. The manufacturer, however, according to a police regulation, must deposit his name and stamp, engraven in copper, at the mayoralty, and enter the bought or sold precious metal ware in the police book of reference.

BELGIUM.

After the precious metal industry had been for a short time free from all legal encroachments of the State, through the effects of the battle near Fleury it came under the power and regulations of the French Republic, and so became subject to the strict law of the 19th Brumaire. This was somewhat altered for the better by a decree of 14th September, 1814;

of which Article 4 declares that thenceforward gold ware shall have as standards—

1. $\frac{918}{1000}$ = 22 carats.
2. $\frac{833}{1000}$ = 20 ,,
3. $\frac{750}{1000}$ = 18 ,,

and silver ware—

1. $\frac{9343}{1000}$ = 11 oz. 5 grs.
2. $\frac{833}{1000}$ = 10 oz.

The cost of testing silver ware of the first standard which is over 120 grammes, was one rappe for 30 grammes; and for spoons, forks, etc., of the same standard, and weighing less than 120 grammes, 5 rappes. Imported silver ware from Germany possessed a standard of $\frac{833}{1000}$; that from France $\frac{800}{1000}$.

If we take the worth of silver coins of $\frac{900}{1000}$ (1 kilogramme silver = 200 francs) as a basis of calculation, we find that a Belgian silver vessel weighing 1 kilogramme, and of $\frac{834}{1000}$ standard, is worth 185,18 francs; a German silver vessel of like weight, and standard of $\frac{833}{1000}$, is worth 180,55 francs; and a French silver vessel of like weight, and $\frac{800}{1000}$, is worth 177,77 francs.

Accordingly, the German silver vessel was 4,63 francs, and the French 7,41 francs cheaper than the Belgian, and sold at that rate in Belgium itself.

The Belgian precious metal industry could not prosper. The export trade between 1858 and 1863 furnished a yearly average of 66,000 francs for gold ware, and of 65,000 francs for silver ware; while the total of the imports, however, reached the value of 162,000 francs for gold ware, and of 258,000 francs for silver ware. In fact, the local industry is far from being able to supply the needs of the inhabitants. In 1861 there were in Belgium 255,180 gold articles stamped, which were either of home or of foreign make, and weighed 702 kilogrammes 828 grammes. Nearly all these had a standard of $\frac{750}{1000}$. Taking the gold of this standard at 2,583 francs a kilogramme, the average value of each article would be 7 francs 11 cents. In the same year there were 329,464 silver articles stamped, which together weighed 6,040 kilogrammes 540 grammes. Supposing these to have been of the legal Belgian standard, viz., $\frac{833\frac{1}{3}}{1000}$, the average value of each article at 185,18 francs per kilogramme would be 3,40 francs. Of 8,657 silver articles, 6,531 were worth on an average 20 rappes each. This shows that precious metal articles of a low price are largely sought for.

The Belgian Finance Minister, on the 19th November, 1867, brought in a bill (accepted by both Houses with some few modifications) of which—

Article 1 declares that the manufacture of precious metal ware is permitted at all standards, and compulsory State control ceases.

Article 2 enables buyers and sellers alike to have the precious metal ware tested as to standard and stamp at the testing office; the standards for gold ware being fixed at $\frac{900}{1000}$ and $\frac{750}{1000}$, and for silver ware at $\frac{900}{1000}$ and $\frac{800}{1000}$.

Article 3 directs that ware of a standard between the two shall receive the stamp of the lower.

Article 4 authorises the buyer of precious metal ware to demand a statement of the weight, standard, price, and other particulars of his purchase; which the seller is thereupon bound to supply.

This bill came into operation on the 1st July,

1869. A clause therein sets forth that the Royal stamp, with the letters O (or) and A (argent), and the figure 1 or 2 for standard, shall be impressed on each article. For legal confirmation of the standard (2) shall be placed on hollow articles, of such character that it can be seen at once that no foreign matter is inserted therein. The cost of testing gold ware is fixed at 10 francs per hectogramme, and half a franc for silver ware; gold ware under one gramme being taxed as *one* gramme, and silver under 10 grammes as for 10 grammes.

The Belgian Finance Minister urged the acceptance of these laws, on the ground that they would free the precious metal industry in Belgium from burdensome restrictions, and showed that the principles implied therein had been productive of the happiest results in Holland and Germany.

HOLLAND.

The law of September 18th, 1852, determined the working of precious metal in each standard.

The guaranteed regulations of the degrees of the standards are as follows :—

Gold Ware.	Silver Ware.
1. $\frac{916}{1000}$	1. $\frac{934}{1000}$
2. $\frac{833}{1000}$	2. $\frac{833}{1000}$
3. $\frac{750}{1000}$	
4. $\frac{583}{1000}$	

Precious metal ware of other standards bears a stamp in token of the payment of the duty required by the State. Moreover, every manufacturer is compelled to place his own stamp on all completed articles.

Gold ware is subject to a duty of 12 florins per hectogramme; and silver ware of 60 cents per hectogramme.

ITALY.

In the kingdom of Italy, with the exception of Tuscany, the law is that the minimum standard of silver ware shall be $\frac{800}{1000}$, and of gold ware $\frac{800}{1000}$.

Before the formation of the kingdom of Italy there were different laws for every State, and different standards.

GOLD.

In Naples the standards were:—

Gold Ware.	Silver Ware.
$\frac{916\frac{2}{3}}{1000}$	$\frac{915\frac{1}{2}}{1000}$
$\frac{833}{1000}$	$\frac{847\frac{1}{2}}{1000}$
$\frac{750}{1000}$	
$\frac{900\frac{1}{2}}{1000}$	
$\frac{883\frac{1}{2}}{1000}$	
$\frac{800}{1000}$	

In the States of the Church:—

Gold Ware.	Silver Ware.
$\frac{916\frac{2}{3}}{1000}$	$\frac{937}{1000}$
$\frac{750}{1000}$	$\frac{875}{1000}$

In Sardinia:—·

Gold Ware.	Silver Ware.
$\frac{840}{1000}$	$\frac{950}{1000}$
$\frac{750}{1000}$	$\frac{800}{1000}$

In Tuscany:—

Gold Ware.	Silver Ware.
$\frac{833\frac{1}{2}}{1000}$	$\frac{987}{1000}$
$\frac{625}{1000}$	$\frac{791\frac{2}{3}}{1000}$
	$\frac{687\frac{1}{2}}{1000}$

In Parma:—-

Gold Ware.	Silver Ware.
$\frac{833\frac{1}{2}}{1000}$	$\frac{917}{1000}$
$\frac{750}{1000}$	$\frac{792}{1000}$

It is evident that the legal restrictions in Italy have operated neither to the advantage of the industry nor to the benefit of the public. In May, 1873, a law came into operation which contains the following clauses :—

Article 1.—Working of gold and silver is permitted in all standards.

Article 2.—When desired, the following standards may be confirmed by stamp in the office for testing gold and silver.

Gold Ware.	Silver Ware.
1. $\frac{900}{1000}$	$\frac{960}{1000}$
2. $\frac{750}{1000}$	$\frac{900}{1000}$
3. $\frac{800}{1000}$	$\frac{800}{1000}$

Article 3.—Precious metals of a standard between two standards are to receive the stamp due to the lower of the two. Only ware of homogeneous character will be stamped.

Article 5.—Royal testing offices shall be established where the industries require it, on condition of the cost of their maintenance in excess of the duties received being guaranteed.

Article 6.—False stamping punishable by law.

Article 7.—If a precious metal ware is fraudulently filled with foreign material, the manufacturer to be imprisoned for one year.

A decree of December, 1872, contains the following :—

GOLD.

Article 2.—There are six standard stamps, three for gold ware and three for silver ware.

For gold, the *first stamp* is a Jupiter head; the *second*, a Minerva profile; and the *third*, a horse's head. While for silver, the three stamps are signified by an Italian turret, with the distinguishing numbers 1, 2, 3.

Article 9.—Articles brought to the office for stamping must either be finished or require only to be polished.

Article 11.—In case of discontent or dissension as to the real standard of a precious metal ware, it may be tested a second time; and, if this be disputed, it must be sent to the central testing office.

Article 13.—An alloy of $\frac{3}{1000}$ is allowed for gold and silver ware.

Article 14.—The duty for testing gold ware is 50 francs per kilo., and for silver ware 5 francs per kilo.

Article 15.—For precious metal ware not answering to any standard nor requiring any stamp, the duty for simply testing is 40 francs for gold, and 4 francs for silver, per kilo. The duty is in no case less than 20 rappes.

Article 20.—All duties are devoted to the good of the State.

Article 27.—The testing officers are bound to complete the testing on the same day the precious metal ware is delivered to them.

Article 30.—The testing officers must stamp the article on the principal part, and not on a subordinate part. If the article consists of several parts which can be separated, it must be stamped on each part.

SPAIN.

The standards for gold ware are :—

    1. $\frac{916\frac{2}{3}}{1000}$ 2. $\frac{833\frac{1}{3}}{1000}$ 3. $\frac{750}{1000}$

And for silver :—

    1. $\frac{916\frac{2}{3}}{1000}$ 2. $\frac{700}{1000}$

PORTUGAL.

The standard for gold ware is $\frac{848\frac{1}{3}}{1000}$, and for silver ware $\frac{833\frac{1}{3}}{1000}$. For bijouterie a lower standard is allowed.

AUSTRIA.

The legal regulations of the standard of precious metal ware were not the same in all parts of the kingdom.

With relation to this question the crown lands were separated into three distinct groups, viz. :—

1st. Deutsch - Sclavischen Ländern (Sclavonia).

2nd. The Lombardo-Venetian kingdom.

3rd. The Hungarian division, including Dalmatia and Cracow.

The differences were as follows :—

The Hungarian division had no laws or restrictions for the standards of gold and silver ware.

In the Lombardo-Venetian kingdom, according to the Napoleonic law of 1810, all gold and silver ware (without exception) was subject to control; while in the Deutsch-Sclavischen territory, according to a law of 1824, gold ware of less weight than 4 ducats was not subject to stamping.

The following standards were observed in the Lombardo-Venetian division :—

Gold ware: 22 carats, 21 carats, 20 carats, and 18 carats.

Silver: 15 ounces and 12 ounces.

In Deutsch-Sclavischen territory (Sclavonia):

Gold ware: 7 carats 10 grains, 13 carats 1 grain, 18 carats 5 grains.

Silver ware: 15 ounces and 13 ounces

The necessity for uniformity of regulations was so evident that in 1835 a discussion was opened, and the issue of a circular explaining the state of the standards determined on; but without any practical results.

The discrepancies between the different groups were so great, and led to such embarrassing results, that the necessity for legislative enactment was acknowledged by the State, and gave rise to the scheme of provisional regulations for stamping the standards of gold and silver ware in 1852. But this also fared the same fate as other endeavours; it never became law.

The first real step towards improvement was caused by the conference of delegates from the Zoll Verein, who, in 1856, devoted ten sittings to the question of " Unanimity in the Control of the Standards of Gold and Silver Ware."

Before proceeding to give the laws now in force, it is worth mention that in Austria at the present time, and under the altered condition of the empire, Vienna is the only great centre of the gold and silver ware industry. There are manufactures in Pressburg, but they are governed by laws of their own, derived from an earlier period, and exempting them from control and duty.

Laws now in force.

1.—The standards of home-manufactured or imported gold and silver ware are subject to the Control Office.

2.—Officers are appointed by the Home Secretary.

3.—A duty to be imposed for the payment of Control.

4.—Standards of gold and silver to be expressed in "thousandths"—$\frac{1}{1000}$.

6.—For convenience of the Control Office, gold and silver ware is divided into *bars*, *wares* (including trinkets, jewellery, chains), *wire*, and objects manufactured from the wire.

7.—All finished gold and silver wares of home manufacture to have the name of the manufacturer stamped on them, and to be deposited in the Control Office for the purpose of testing their standards.

10.—Bars to receive the stamp of the Control Office, and the standard to be expressed in figures.

11.—Duty for gold bars, 1 gulden a lb. weight; and silver, half a gulden for like weight. Above 5 lb. weight, half the sum per lb.

13.—Imported bars, having the stamp of a well-known authority, and the standard in plain figures upon them, will not be subject to duty or control.

14.—Gold and silver ware not permitted to be manufactured of a lower standard than that expressed in No. 20.

15.—All new ware to be subject to the Control Officers for stamping and testing.

16.—All goods must have the name of the manufacturer stamped on them; and, if not *quite* finished when taken to the Control Office, must be so nearly so as to exclude the possibility

GOLD.

of tampering with the articles after they have been stamped.

20. Standards for home-manufactured gold and silver ware :—

GOLD WARE.

Standard.		Carats.	Grains.
1. $\frac{916}{1000}$	=	22	0·96
2. $\frac{840}{1000}$	=	20	1·92
3. $\frac{750}{1000}$	=	18	0·
4. $\frac{580}{1000}$	=	13	11·04

SILVER WARE.

Standard.		Ounces.	Grains.
1. $\frac{950}{1000}$	=	15	3·6
2. $\frac{900}{1000}$	=	14	7·2
3. $\frac{800}{1000}$	=	12	14·4
4. $\frac{750}{1000}$	=	12	0·

21. Gold-plated silver articles will be stamped as silver.

Gold and silver plated articles, it is to be understood, do not mean other metals merely plated with gold and silver; which cannot be sold as cheap gold and silver ware.

22. As alloy for gold, only silver or copper may be used; and for silver, only copper. All other metals are forbidden.

47. All workmen in gold and silver ware are bound to give notice to the Control Office on entering on new work, and to communicate any further change.

50. Gold and silver manufacturers or dealers, on retiring from business or making any change, must give notice within eight days of the same, and deliver up their stamps to the office.

The stamp for bar-gold is a royal eagle, and the name of the office where stamped.

The standard stamps for large ware are mythological figures. For gold, the head of Phœbus Apollo, with the Sun's rays; and for silver ware, the head of Diana, with the Moon-sickle.

RUSSIA.

1. To insure the real worth of circulating gold and silver, whether in bars or as ware, it must have the legal sign or stamp.

52. Officers of the testing office are not allowed to carry on any trade connected with the office in which they are employed; nor, either in their own name or in that of any other, to trade in gold and silver; nor to have any

GOLD.

dealings with master manufacturers, jewellers, or gold and silversmiths.

71. Standards for gold ware and bars :—

$$\frac{6\,6}{9\,6} \qquad \frac{7\,2}{9\,6} \qquad \frac{8\,2}{9\,6} \qquad \frac{9\,1}{9\,6}$$

Gold used for soldering is required to be not lower than $\frac{3\,8}{9\,6}$; silver for the same purpose must not be below $\frac{8\,4}{9\,6}$.

Standards for silver and for gold plated :—

$$\frac{8\,4}{9\,6} \qquad \frac{8\,8}{9\,6} \qquad \frac{9\,1}{9\,6}$$

72. As alloy for gold, only red copper or silver may be used; and for silver, only red copper.

76. Russian coins, native gold, gold-sand, and unstamped bars are not allowed to be melted together.

107. Trade in gold and silver ware of every kind, and bars, may be conducted in open magazines and shops, either exclusively or in conjunction with other articles. But it is strictly forbidden to sell them in little huts, or on stalls in the market-place.

114. All who desire to work in the gold trade, in whatever branch it may be, must obtain permission; and this permission must be renewed in the December of every year.

120. No gold and silver worker can change his place of occupation without notice and without permission.

SWITZERLAND.

Canton Basle.—1. All gold and silver manufacturers must be most accurate in ascertaining and providing that the standard for gold ware is 18 carats, and for silver, 12 oz. 9 grs.

2. All finished articles must have the name of the goldsmith stamped on them.

3. Every master whose name is stamped on the article is answerable for its standard, whether it was made here or in other lands.

There is not a large industry of gold and silver ware in Basle, most of the ware being imported from Paris and Geneva.

Canton Zurich.—Standard for gold, 18 carats; and for silver, 13 oz. 6 deniers.

There are three manufactories for gold and silver ware in this Canton; viz., at Zurich, Winterthur, and Elgg.

Canton Soleure.—No real laws existing.

Canton Glarus.—No new law has been enacted since 1761, when the standard was fixed for silver at 12 oz.; but nothing said of gold.

Lucerne, 1804.—1. Neither gold nor silver manufacturer may sell ware under 18-carat standard for gold, and 13 oz. for silver.

5. Gold and silver ware sent out without the name of the manufacturer and the arms of the Canton, will be confiscated to the State, and a fine of sixteen francs imposed upon the manufacturer.

Wardens are appointed to inspect the several workshops and the yearly markets, and to report to the President of the Canton.

Pays de Vaud.—Up to 1848 there was no law regulating the standard of gold and silver ware; but in December of that year it was decreed—

1. All precious metal ware manufactured or sold in the Pays de Vaud must have the correct standard.

4. For gold ware—$\frac{760}{1000}$.

5. For silver—$\frac{900}{1000}$ and $\frac{800}{1000}$.

6. It is expressly forbidden to sell ware in the Canton or out of it of lower standard than Article 5 expresses.

12. Every article must be stamped with the

name of the manufacturer and the degree of the standard.

14. The Chamber of Commerce is appointed to watch over the standard of the precious metals in the Pays de Vaud.

15. Every gold or silversmith must deposit his stamp at the Chamber of Commerce; and this Chamber must see that every manufacturer has a different stamp.

16. Should the manufacturer die, or his business be given up, his stamp is broken up at the Chamber of Commerce.

24. Strange merchants buying precious metal ware at the market of this Canton must give notice to the Chamber of Commerce, in order that the ware may be tested.

25. When the testers are about to inspect the ware, they have to take an oath before a Commissioner of the Chamber of Commerce.

In November, 1873, permission was granted for the manufacture of precious metal ware at any standard the manufacturer may be pleased to adopt.

In 1874 gold ware was required to have $\frac{840}{1000}$ standard; and silver, $\frac{800}{1000}$.

. If a wrong stamp be placed on the ware, a

GOLD.

fine is inflicted of from 30 to 500 francs, or imprisonment from 10 to 180 days.

Canton Neufchatel.—The oldest laws in this Canton concerning the precious metal industry date from September, 1754.

Manufacturers are forbidden to make gold ware under 18 carats, and silver ware under 13 ounces.

Of confiscated goods, a third goes to the King of Prussia, a third to the officers, and a third to the informer who discovered the fraud.

Canton Geneva.—The principal industry is watch-making and bijouterie.

Manufacturing here is permitted at all standards; but the gold ware must not be lower than $\frac{750}{1000}$, nor the silver lower than $\frac{800}{1000}$.

The remaining Cantons have no laws relating to gold and silver ware.

SWEDEN.

In Sweden there are three standards for gold ware, viz.: ducat-gold, pistolen-gold, and crown-gold; or 23 carat 5 gr., 20 carat 4 gr., and 18 carat 4 gr.

All goods, except the very small, must be stamped.

NORWAY.

No gold ware can be sold that has not a standard of from 18 to 14 carats, at the lowest; and all must be stamped by the manufacturer, and bear the standard stamp.

PRUSSIA.

No restrictive laws in force.

BAVARIA.

Minimum standard of gold ... $\frac{580}{1000}$
,, ,, silver ... $\frac{800}{1000}$.

SAXONY.

No new laws; and the old ones not enforced.

HESSE.

Since 1829 all gold and silversmiths are compelled to have their ware stamped with the standard, the initials of the manufacturer, and the arms of the Duchy.

MECKLENBURG-STRELITZ.

No new laws since 1572; and those not enforced.

OLDENBURG.

A law of 1760 declares that the standard for silver is to be 12 oz.; and that, together with the name of the manufacturer, must be stamped on it.

BRUNSWICK.

Name and standard to be marked on goods, on pain of 20 thalers fine or imprisonment.

HAMBURG.

No silver can have a less standard than 11 oz. 12 grs. All ware of a higher standard to be stamped with the maker's name and the standard.

There is no law in Hamburg for gold ware.

BREMEN.

Never had any restrictive laws for precious metal trade.

LÜBECK.

Previous to 1872 no silver ware could be made in this town under a standard of 12 oz. to the mark. Since that period, however, permission has been given to manufacture of any standard.

All goods to be stamped at the cost of the manufacturer.

In other lands and towns of Europe no restrictive laws exist.

AMERICA.

There are no special statutes concerning the standard of articles made from the precious metals, either in the United States or in the States of South America.

EGYPT.

Laws like those of Turkey.

MOROCCO.

Laws like those of France.

CHINA.

Nothing but *pure gold* is allowed to be worked here; and any Chinaman found alloying the precious metal in order to deceive the purchaser, is *decapitated*.

PERSIA.

There are no restrictions on the manufacture of precious metal ware.

In Germany a common legislative regulation of the standard of gold and silver ware has already been adverted to. The transactions most fresh in our remembrance, however, are those of the year 1856, which we have sketched above, and which were intended to lead to a regulation of the standard of gold and silver ware in association with Austria, and upon the principle proposed by that State.

Notwithstanding this, no common legislation resulted; but on the 21st June, 1869, a trade order was issued, which put an end to the existence of the guild by which the limitations of the standard of gold and silver had hitherto been defined. However, in certain towns of Germany (Berlin, for example) may still be found testers appointed and sworn by the Goldsmiths' Corporation; nor is the influence of the guild by any means extinguished, since in Berlin (where silver only is stamped, and that simply in a facultative manner) a tester, appointed by the guild, marks the standard only upon such articles as are at least of 12 oz. quality.

These remnants of old rights, the exercise of which is slowly continued like an ineradicable disease, still give character to the laws upon the precious metal trade in such towns as from the nature of their industry stand prominently forward in this department.

Silver ware of 11 oz. standard weight is therefore chiefly manufactured in Schleswig, Holstein, Posen, and Silesia; of 12 oz. in the northern and eastern parts of Germany; and of 13 oz. standard in the southern and western parts.

In the meantime "the competition as to price, and the abuses resulting from loose laws of protection, which are evaded or transgressed with impunity, have lowered the standards of silver by admitting an excess of alloy, which, if not corrected, will render the name of 'German Silver' synonymous abroad with adulterated and spurious metal."

These are the words of a petition of October 4th, 1872, addressed by 154 silver manufacturers of North and South Germany to the Confederation and Diet, to which undoubtedly belongs the credit of having called attention afresh to the common regulation of the standard of gold and silver ware in the German Empire. There, however, the credit of the petition ends, for it seeks to lay restrictions upon the silver trade which are in open opposition to the principles of national freedom.

The proposed law, subjoined to this petition, runs as follows :—

1. From the 1st January, 1874, silver articles may not be manufactured in the German empire, or imported from abroad, which have a lower standard than that of the weight of 800 in 1,000 parts. Every other protective enact-

ment, except that hitherto conceded to the Mint, is repealed.

2. The standard is to be indicated by a stamp, viz., an imperial crown with an eagle or similar device, and the number 800 placed against it. This stamp to be manufactured in Berlin, and to be issued by the local authorities on the expenses being defrayed by the manufacturer or seller. All silver goods to be impressed with the stamp. Should these have a standard in excess of 800, it is to be expressed in decimals beside the imperial stamp.

3. Silver ware of lower standard, in hand at the time of the introduction of this law, may be sold out, but they are not to be furnished with the imperial stamp.

4. Every seller of silver ware is to be obliged to place his trade-mark beside the imperial stamp, and undertakes in so doing to guarantee to the buyer the right standard. If the seller be not himself the manufacturer, he can make the latter responsible should an investigation prove a defective standard. The last buyer, however, has the right to claim against the person who sold to him. If a seller will not undertake this responsibility, he may not stamp

his own trade-mark; but in that event he must indicate that of the working silversmith or manufacturer, so that the buyer may always enjoy a personal security in addition to that implied in the imperial stamp.

5. In doubtful cases assayers appointed by the German Mints are commissioned to investigate the silver goods submitted to them, in conformity with the process pursued in the coinage. Should the investigation disclose an inferior standard, the seller or the manufacturer (as the case may be) must pay the penalty imposed by law.

The fact of so large a number as 154 men in the trade expressing themselves in favour of this law may induce others to favour it also. We are not unaware that in all national reforms, the advantages of which were patent from the first, it has always been those most concerned who have been slowest to perceive them.

An imposing number of silver manufacturers send up a petition, ostensibly for reform; but it really proves to be nothing better than a generalization of already existing restraints; or an advocacy of laws to limit the freedom of manufacture. But that this restriction is adverse to the manufacture may be illustrated by the success which has attended the repeal of the laws on gold and silver in the case of Geneva and other States; the benefit extending beyond the special sphere of the trade to the wider compass of the whole nation.

PART III.

HAS the statesman to deal with the gold trade and with the silver trade in the same manner, or in a different manner?

The above-mentioned petition was signed by *silver* manufacturers alone. Why do not the manufacturers of gold demand the same measures? The petitioners themselves give the reason for their abstinence. Although they would most willingly (says the petition) have laid before the Confederation a scheme for legislation upon gold ware also, they were not able to obtain proposals for the same from the principal manufacturers of gold ware in Pforzheim, Stuttgart, and Hanover, because the legal treatment of this branch of trade presents much greater difficulties. The small size of the objects seems to render it impossible that they should bear a distinct stamp; in the case of the greater number of gold ware, the value of the pure metal is of much less significance, in proportion to the price of the article, than in the case of silver ware; and the value of the metal is by many jewellers made quite subordinate to the setting (the best setting) for stones or pearls. Lastly, a very important export trade in cheap gold articles has arisen in Germany, which would be injured if in Germany itself interruptions were placed in the way of sale by legal enactments as to standards.

These grounds of opposition only prove that the disadvantages bound up with legal restrictions upon the commerce in precious metals are more apparent with regard to gold than to silver ware. No sound reason, however, exists to require that the trade in silver ware should be dealt with differently from the trade in gold manufactures. It is true that, generally speaking, it is easier to place a stamp upon silver ware than upon gold ware; yet there are many silver articles, such as rings, chains, and filagree

F

work, which either cannot be stamped at all, or only with great difficulty. Further, the small value of the metal in many gold articles can be no reason for passing over the great number in which the value of the metal is very considerable; and thirdly, as to the injury which the export trade in gold ware would suffer through a government regulation of the standard, this applies equally to the case of silver ware.

" The trade of Pforzheim," writes the Chamber of Commerce in that town, " owes its existence and its present extent to its deliverance from every impediment in the form of decrees as to the standard of the manufactured gold. It is by this means that it is in a position to manufacture for all parts of the world, and to adapt itself to the requirements of trade." If it be true, then, that the saleability of all ware depends principally upon the skill with which the manufacturer suits the tastes of the purchasers, can any reason be found why the freedom so advantageous to the German gold manufacture should be considered injurious to the so closely connected trade in silver ware?

We have heard of yet another ground for supporting a separate legislative treatment of the trades in gold and in silver ware. The Swabian Chamber of Trade and Commerce affirms, according to this year's "Alte Algemeine Zeitung" of the 9th of March, in the judgment sent in to the Bavarian government upon the legal regulation of the standard of gold and silver ware, that important authorities had pointed out that in many of the uses to which silver is applied, particularly in utensils for food, a lower standard than that of $\frac{800}{1000}$ acts in a manner injurious to health. So long, however, as these "important authorities" remain unknown, we may be allowed to doubt their assertion, as regards the utensils for food. And what other silver utensils could by any possibility act in a manner injurious to health? The only injurious substance which might be formed in the use of spoons containing copper, is the so-called "verdigris."

The formation of verdigris from an acid and fine copper is, however, a very slow process; so that food must have been immersed for days in an acid fermentation, and a spoon for a still longer time, before the formation of verdigris could take place. Verdigris might be formed rather more quickly from the contact of silver articles with very acid food; but even in this case an injurious effect would result only from very great want of cleanliness, and from the utensil in question being allowed to remain unwashed for a considerable time. Even when we have taken these exceptional conditions into account, still it does not appear why the exact standard of $\frac{800}{1000}$ should form the boundary at which all danger of poisoning disappears; and even were this the boundary, it would by no means follow that it would be beneficial to prescribe for all silver goods (for instance, watch-cases) such a minimum standard.

In this case, which we by no means consider as proved, it would be necessary that police directions should be published on the subject; *but no reason exists why legislation should deal with the whole silver trade otherwise than it does with the gold trade.*

Besides, it is but seldom that one of the trades in precious metals has been exempted, while the burdensome attentions of the statesman and the tax-gatherer have been at the same time bestowed upon the other.

PART IV.

HAS experience been favourable to legal regulations as to exact standards of precious metal ware, or the contrary?

" By their fruits ye shall know them." If we glance over an epitome of the laws which in the states of Europe treat of the precious metal trade, and if we consider that in almost every small country one law has been superseded by another because each has been insufficient to attain its object, and how this again has been supplemented by a second, third, fourth, and so on continually, we shall feel inclined at once to pronounce in favour of freedom in this department of national economy.

We know that in the Canton of Neufchatel, during a period of 119 years (from 1754 to 1873), *thirteen laws* were framed; in France, during a period of 332 years (1506 to 1838), *forty-three laws* were framed; and in England, during a period of 616 years (from 1238 to 1854), *fifty-six laws* were framed, which altered more or less the standard of precious metals. We see, therefore, that it was found necessary to alter the laws relating to the standard of precious metal ware during the periods just mentioned, in Neufchatel every nine years, in France every seven years, and in England every eleven years. This is only the number of which information has come down to us. Were the whole number known to us, the failure of legislation upon this subject would be far more plainly manifested.

Experience, therefore, has pronounced throughout in this matter against the interference of the State.

But we are far from holding by the false principle that "to experiment is better than to study." Let us rather endeavour by deductive reasoning to obtain the *truth*.

PART V.

CAN the legal regulations of the standard of precious metal ware be justified by deductive reasoning?

Two motives have existed to induce legislators to subject the precious metal trade to legal restrictions.

Either the Exchequer felt that no more fitting object of taxation could be found than the ornaments of the rich ; or economists have demanded that the State should here exercise its power : oftener, indeed, both motives have ruled at the same time, as in France, for example, until now. Thanks to the financial position of the German empire, however, we have to deal only with the second motive.

The first question is : Are there any valid grounds for demanding different legal regulations for the trade in precious metal ware from those applied to all other trades, which—with slight exceptions—have the right of manufacturing goods of any quality ?

Among the exceptions here adverted to, the Government control of chemists' shops stands foremost. Next comes the legal testing of firearms, which has been introduced in Belgium and in other countries also. It should be further mentioned that in Great Britain the anchors and anchor-chains of every British ship must be tested at a legally authorised place. Attention should be turned to the fact that in these exceptions it is the *life* or *health* of the purchaser which comes under consideration, whereas in the precious metals trade it is his *interest* only that is concerned. Though there certainly are other instances of State interference in behalf of the well-being or the interest of the purchaser, it must not be overlooked that to every such exercise of State control objections may be raised, and indeed have been raised, which are entitled to consideration. Thus the necessity for the control of weights and measures might seem to one (without pronouncing judgment upon the measure) to be reduced by the fact of the gradual adoption of a more scientific system of cookery, which obliges heads of households to provide themselves with scales and measures for the purpose of maintaining a check upon tradesmen.

The control of weights and measures, of firearms, anchor-chains, apothecaries' shops, and other productions of trade, is a remnant of times gone by, in which the manufacture of a far greater number of goods than at present was subjected to the supervision of the State. Thus, in the thread and linen patents granted to Bohemia, Moravia, and Silesia, in the years

1724, 1750, and 1755, minute directions were given as to the quality of these products, even their length and breadth being specified; and the paper regulation of 1754 determined the weight of each description of paper, and particularised its length and breadth.

The decrees relating to weaving were of a similar character; and those as to the quality of silk goods, light cloth, and velvet manufactures, issued in the middle of the last century, were conceived in the same spirit.

If, however, the removal of legal restrictions may be rightly called the chief characteristic of national progress; if the most important laws of modern times in the civilized states of Europe have originated nothing, but have rather renewed old decrees, how cogent must be the reasons which could induce the legislators of to-day to impose new restrictions. In any case, few will be willing to adopt the principle that the *rule* shall be formed upon the failure of legal restrictions upon trade, and the justification mainly indicated by exceptional cases. The question of the legal regulation of the trade in precious metals will therefore have to be judged by the *rule;* and those who approve of Government restrictions will have to sift to the bottom their reasons for the exceptional ground on which they rely.

What are these reasons ?

Let us take the bull by the horns.

The chief consideration alleged in behalf of the legal regulation of the standard of gold and silver wares, and which underlies most of the attempts made to justify this usurpation of power by the State on the ground of prudence, is the circumstance that gold and silver are also applied to the coinage of money.

The horns of the bull with which we have here to contend vanish like an empty phantom when one reflects that this circumstance is a purely accidental one, and that this accident does not furnish the smallest justification for the legal regulation of the standard of precious metal ware. It is true that it might have appeared convenient to the legislators of centuries gone by, in which the alloy of precious metals was not so well understood as to-day, to provide by law that the precious metal utensils of the country should have the same standard as the coins, so that the trouble might be avoided of altering the standard of the utensils when melted down before the test could be applied to the coinage of money. But to-day, when the art of refining and alloy has made such great progress, if we adopt this argument of our forefathers as our *own*, a representation is advanced as to the part played by precious metals in our national economy which we do not hesitate to designate as doubtful and misleading to an astonishing degree. And yet this justification of the legal regulation of the standard of precious metal ware recurs in almost every case in which such a regulation is recommended. Indeed, to speak quite plainly, the chief reason (in our opinion) why so little energy has been manifested on behalf of freeing the precious metal ware from legal restrictions, and of upholding its freedom, is because the State stamps the sign of its authority upon gold and silver coins; a circumstance which seems to confuse the judgment. Because it happens that neither precious stones nor any other materials are made use of as money, the multitude cries, Let gold and silver be considered holy! Let them bear, in whatever form they may appear, the mark of the State! Very well; now we shall see that the stamp of the State upon precious metal ware may prove to be a mark of Cain; nay, that it often is such.

With no more leniency than we show to the supporters of this much valued argument for the legal regulation of the standard of precious metal ware, shall we judge those who base their defence of its regulation by the State upon the necessity of maintaining its character as a measure of value.

It is very easy to see that one could not possess in gold rings or plate an absolute measure of value if the manufacture of such articles, in all standards, were permitted. It would be necessary, therefore, to fall back on the position which but few States have ventured to take up, viz., that only one standard should be authorised.

It is very evident, and the experience of other States has also proved, that legal restriction leads to the most serious disadvantages. It lays the greatest possible difficulties in the way of the requirements of trade and the gratification of the public. It hinders the export of the produce of native industry, and any attempt to enforce its regulations must lead to measures for watching over the customs; for the transgression of a legal restriction attended by so many evil consequences may be regarded as matter of course.

Apart from all these evil consequences, however, it is to be observed that the necessity of insisting upon relief from the legal restriction of the standard of precious metal ware to *one* degree still exists.

In earlier times gold and silver ware often supplied the place of the means of exchange, which were then scarce. In this way the English country nobleman, who had no money for his parliamentary journey to London, gave his plate to the nearest goldsmith, who, in return, provided him with a letter of credit to a London goldsmith—at that time a London banker. Now, however, in no civilized country is there any lack of means of exchange. Where, then, lies the necessity of multiplying the materials of exchange?

But the public will be protected! Gold and silver, it is argued, are amongst the most costly of ware, and here or nowhere should the State protect us from fraud. Let the State, then, do its duty. The costliness of gold and silver is an argument for the proposed demand which will not hold good. For why should the public be found to require protection in the purchase of ware precisely of the value of gold and silver? Why not in the purchase of wares which, at the same weight, are of *higher* value? for instance, in the purchase of diamonds? Why not, also, in the purchase of ware, the value of which, at like weight, lies *between* the value of gold and silver; as, for instance, in the purchase of lace? Or, again, why not in the purchase of ware, the value of which, at the same weight, lies *below* the value of silver?

It has been further stated that the public should especially receive protection from the State in the purchase of precious metal ware, because the public is not sufficiently competent in the matter to be guarded against the salesman. If this principle holds good, to what mass of wares would it apply! For example, how great is the difference between real and imitation champagne; between genuine and imitation lace; between good and bad cloth; between good and bad clocks; between real stones and paste; between real pearls and glass imitations; between good spectacles and bad, &c., &c. How difficult it is for the layman at times to exercise a correct judgment upon these wares, and yet it never occurs to us to call in the aid of the State in making a purchase of any one of them. Do we depend, then, upon the honour of the seller? By no means; but upon the recognition the latter has of his own advantage, which will prevent him from placing in jeopardy the custom, not only of one person, but of all.

There is, therefore, not the smallest ground for calling in State aid, in making our purchases of gold and silver.

With regard to the defence of legal regulation of precious metal ware, in the form of compulsion to alloy the upper and middle standards, *that it will lead at last to impossibility of manufacturing precious metal wares of very low standard, whose worth is lost with the destruction of the form of the article;* even this ground for the proposal under consideration does not hold good, in our opinion. It implies that the small quantities of gold and silver which escape by friction in the mechanical working of these metals *are lost;* but this is not true, except as to infinitesimally small particles. For buyers of old gold and silver at the highest price are always to be met with; and anyone having a remnant of a chain or other trinket, of however low a standard, can always sell it. This is owing to the fact that the art of refining has advanced at a great rate, insomuch that one nowadays is able to extract minute specks of gold and silver even out of the most heterogeneous matter. The goldsmiths are accustomed to sweep their workshops out once a year, or thereabout, and to send the sweepings to so-called refiners, that the gold and silver dust may be extracted by them.

In the next place, the widest possible extension of the use of precious metal ware, which is paralyzed by legal restrictions but encouraged by freedom, is to be regarded as advantageous to the wealth of the people; because we must remember, that the trade in gold and silver ware represents one of the most suitable investments of superfluous capital. In the purchase of precious metal ware, a satisfactory result is ensured to both of those aims which it is usual to keep in view in the investment of capital— viz., *security* and proportionate interest. The best security, at all events, of the investment of a limited capital is, as in this instance, the possession of one's own property; while the interest is fully represented in the beautifying of existence which we owe to gold and silver ornaments and gold and silver plate. Since the public takes so much pleasure in precious metal ware, such an outlay of capital obtains the importance of a very alluring investment for spare cash. The use of precious metal ware, so loudly decried, positively serves to augment the savings of a nation.

Orientals, therefore, and all other nations who are not able to invest their capital with security, have done well to decide upon investing it in precious stones and gold and silver ornaments. "And yet," as Count von Moltke, with much insight into national economy, remarks, "such nations indicate by the very abundance of their ornaments how poor is their wealth as a nation."

However, they have made a virtue of necessity.

As a further argument in support of the fact that the use of precious metal ware is conducive to the wealth of a nation, we may add, that in proportion to the hold obtained by precious metal ware will the sale of ornamental goods made of the inferior metals and low qualities of gold diminish.

The working power is therefore preserved to the nation, which would otherwise be wasted in the manufacture of trifles.

It is to be further noted that ornaments made of precious metals are generally preserved with greater care than the perishable, worthless goods, known under the name of "Quincaillerie," and also that fashion is far less capricious in jewellery than in these less important articles.

Whoever possesses a golden ornament, if of 18-carat gold, knows himself to be worth its value, £3 3s. 8½d. per oz. He is independent of the mutations of fashion.

Few people are in a position, or even have the wish, to be guided by the fashions of the gold and silver manufactures. On the contrary, in many families old-fashioned silver is used in preference.

If Government regulation of the standard of gold and silver is defensible neither on the ground that gold and silver are also made use of as money, nor because silver plate formerly answered as a measure of value, nor because the public either claim protection on account of the high value of precious metal goods, or have a difficulty in deciding the standards, nor, finally, because advantage might accrue to the wealth of the nation, then, on the whole, it is not required at all. For no other arguments have been produced in favour of legal regulation in this department; and we claim to have proved that no reason exists for deviating from the *rule* in this particular of gold and silver ware, which rule is the *non-interference of the State with trade.* If we ask the reader to follow us still further, it is because we are convinced that the public, in the formation of its views, is not decisively influenced by the evidence of *non-justification.* Let us, therefore, return to experiment, and assume that neither the inductive proof which we sought to establish in Section 4, nor yet the deductive method argued in this section, has overthrown the principle of legal regulation of the standard of gold and silver ware; and let us ask :—

PART VI.

WHAT methods have been applied or proposed in order to render possible the legal regulation of the standard of gold and silver wares; and what actual or conjectural results does the application of these methods yield?

Those Government rules which lay upon the manufacturers of gold and silver ware a compulsory degree of one or more standards are called, in the Austrian reports, *Imperative-preventive Control;* and, for the practical working of this control, Government offices are erected for the purpose of testing the manufactured gold and silver wares, and of providing them with the Government stamp. This is the system employed in Austria.

The authorities at the Imperial Stamping Office in Vienna have had the goodness to supply us with a statistical report of the precious metal ware which had passed through the office in Austria from 1867 to 1873.

This report shows that the entire weight of stamped precious metal ware increased from '67 to '72, but decreased in '73. The entire weight stamped of gold and silver in lbs. troy for these several years is as follows :—

	Gold Ware.	Silver Ware.
1867	3143·6715	33904·412
1868	5718·0020	56516·526
1869	6915·4038	60480·822
1870	6868·5030	58709·914
1871	8566·5005	70992·130
1872	10353·8170	91783·805
1873	10223·9881	87067·221

The director, in sending these figures, remarks :—" It is to be concluded, from the dates contained in this statement, that the present stamp law of the Imperative-preventive Control, and the principle on which it is grounded, have had a very serviceable influence upon the development of the gold and silver trade, and upon the credit of the Austrian gold and silver ware."

Upon this we must observe that, to all appearance, the figures embrace the foreign as well as the home-stamped precious metal ware, and that therefore no conclusion can be drawn from them as to the influence *of the system upon the precious metal trade of Austria.**

Supposing even that in these figures the precious metal ware coming from abroad was not included, still the increase of the entire weight of precious metal ware stamped in Austria under the control system has to be considered side by side with the rise or increase of the same trade in other lands, where the

---

* On inquiring again at the Imperial Chief Stamping Office, we learnt that in the above numbers the precious metal ware coming from abroad *is* included. The amount in pounds weight of those imported from abroad and stamped in Austria is as follows:—

	Gold Ware.	Silver Ware.
1867	783·7556	2893·683
1868	1691·0118	9139·193
1869	1989·8474	10580·975
1870	1880·0835	9675·017
1871	2531·4575	11974·675
1872	3045·0834	15482·085
1873	2985·0738	16600·028

According to these tables the entire weight of the stamped gold plate of *home* manufacture multiplied itself in these years by 3, and silver plate by $2\frac{1}{6}$; while, on the other hand, the imported gold plate by $3\frac{2}{6}$, and the silver plate by $5\frac{7}{10}$. These facts throw a keen ray of light upon the Austrian precious metal trade under the present favourite legislation of standards, and serve as anything rather than a proof of the fruitful influence of the latter.

GOLD. 103

control system is different. And that the import of foreign ware must and does play a considerable part in Austria is proved by the following notice of a member of the Chamber of Commerce, in the year 1871. The Secretary of the Chamber of Commerce, who has sent it to us, tells us that the views contained in it may still be relied upon.

The stamp law, which came into operation on the 1st of January, 1867, from which the tradesmen of Vienna fully anticipated a permanent rise of business, has not fulfilled their expectations; but rather produced all the disadvantages which were predicted by us at the time in repeatedly-delivered opinions.

Foreign competition, the suppression of which was the real motive of the Viennese petitioners in demanding an official stamping, while the protection of the public from fraud was the ostensible pretext, is more active than before; and the import increases visibly, because the trade of Pforzheim, Gmunden, and Hanau very soon accommodated itself to the Austrian stamping directions.

Besides, as was easy to foresee, the importer of manufactured goods has a considerable advantage over the home producer, when one remembers the vexatious determinations of the law : which can be, or rather must be, carried out in the case of the home productions, but which cannot be closely observed in the finished goods.

The importer, again, risks nothing in the attempt to introduce goods contrary to prescription, except the return of the same, while the home producer has all goods of insufficient standard destroyed ; by which operation he becomes a loser to the extent of the cost of their manufacture.

Home trade is further confined to the large towns principally; generally to Vienna and Prague, where the law is carried out in well-organized offices by officials trained to the business. But in the smaller towns, where gold and silver-workers are installed as chief testers (of whom, to say the least, we may assert that they are not trained to the work), much ware is passed for the importer which does not comply with the law, and with which the home manufacturer cannot compete. This, however, is not the place to consider this point more closely, nor would the removal of the disadvantages be practicable even if we could; for the Government cannot establish well-arranged stamping offices in all such places without keeping upon their paid staff a large number of insufficiently occupied officials, and so largely increasing the burdens.

In the Hungarian countries, also, the law appears not to be of advantage to the native industry, for it is practically impossible to compete in Hungary with the wares of Pforzheim, where it is difficult to meet with ware answering to the legal prescriptions, even among that legally imported. These are expressive facts, the causes of which are not difficult to discover.

The first of the numerous difficulties which can be raised against the compulsory control of the State consists in the question whether the charges inseparable from the enactment of such regulations bear any proportion to the advantages, if any such were possible, that the public receive against fraud. These charges are in many countries very large. None are so small as in Lucerne, where *each* of the two testers receives yearly the sum of four francs.

In Austria, in 1867, the testing fees were 76,049 florins; and in 1871 they were 168,758 florins. But far more heavily than the figures of cost do the prohibitive regulations weigh, which are inseparably connected with the imperative preventive control of the standard.

These regulations find expression in two different ways. First, there is the fact that compulsory preventive control can only promise a good result if at the same time precautions are taken that no precious metal wares be imported which have a lower standard than that fixed for home manufacture. Otherwise home industry would be prejudiced in the highest degree. Consequently, compulsory preventive control by the State must inevitably be followed by protective regulations directed against foreign competition in the interest of home industry; and thence arises the disadvantage that the public will be able, neither at home nor abroad, to provide itself with precious metal ware to its liking.

Secondly, compulsory preventive control has had the disadvantage in many countries—France, for example—of compelling the framers of the law to define certain degrees of standard for precious metal ware destined for exportation. How can this be done? If of the same standards as for home, the good repute of the precious metal ware abroad is lost; and, if this be their sole object, the unfairness to those at home is evident. But however this may be, it is clearly perceptible that legal regulations which confine an industry so closely in the chains lead to the most obnoxious results. If the framers of the law prescribe certain standards for precious metal ware destined for abroad, then the precious metal industry is forced into deceptive courses which must lead them, in the natural order of things, to deviate from these regulations. As, however, the interests of one industry cannot be disconnected from those of the whole community, it follows that, if the precious metal industry descend to deceptive and crooked ways, the whole collective industries of the country suffer with it, and are equally degraded.

As a further disadvantage connected with compulsory preventive control, we must cite the fact that manufacturers of precious metal ware could not escape burdensome oppression from the application of control of this kind. Least of all will those manufacturers escape who do not live in the great centres of this industry. As it is impossible to have control establishments in all places, they must either send their ware to the nearest control office, often with serious loss of time and money, not to mention the great risk, or else seek a dwelling in the neighbourhood of a control office. Quite apart from the sacrifices which must result to individual manufacturers, the framers of the law give rise to a grouping of industries of this nature—a grouping which cannot be for the interests of the country. This aspect of the question, however, is of much less importance in the case of the precious metal industry than in that of other crafts, since the head-quarters of the goldsmiths' art have always been confined to the seats of riches and luxury, and therefore to very few places.

It would be a disadvantage of the most serious kind to compel the goldsmiths of small towns to shift their quarters to the departmental capitals, or to give up their occupation, since for many of them there would be no alternative, Again, the buyer of a gold or silver article, if he live in a small town without a control station, will have to give a larger sum for it than if he bought it in one of the larger towns, because the expense of the transit of the article backward and forward to the office has to be made good to the manufacturer; and therefore the buyer will prefer to make his selection in the capital, where he will have a greater choice and less expense.

In spite of the fact that those gold and silversmiths who live in the centre of their craft enjoy the possible advantage of having a control office on the spot, they are beset by manifold burdens in consequence of compulsory preventive control. For it is quite clear that extraordinary laws have no prospect of being obeyed unless they are accompanied by extraordinary means of enforcement. Hence we find—in France, for example—institutions for the inspection of shops and workshops, of the burdensome nature of which we need offer no proof, the character of the system being sufficiently indicated by its name.

The petition of the German silver manufacturers, which has been often referred to, ignores the rules which would be necessary to secure the execution of the proposed law. It is evident, however, that although it would be scarcely possible to introduce an inspector of shops and workshops in the German empire, still the control offices in the three great neighbouring states of the empire could not well be dispensed with if legislation were to decide upon making a definite degree of standard compulsory. Were it desirable to renounce the control offices, it must be observed that the State cannot avoid heavy punishments for the transgression of its laws upon standard, if the law is not to remain a dead letter. But then what a Government rod would the persons who signed the petition in question have laid up for themselves! The wish was to gather roses, but their thorns were forgotten. A workman whose time is precious, and who has not at hand the can containing gold of the standard demanded by law, makes use (perhaps *merely* through error) of gold of a lower standard. Where is here the boundary between oversight and fraud? Might not a similar case happen to every manufacturer of precious metal ware? Does not each one, then, stand daily in danger, not only of being sentenced to severe punishment, but of injury to the highly-prized reputation of his firm? Should it be answered that, in the case of a general manufacturer of one standard only, such an error could not be possible, yet it is not beyond the region of possibility that a workman might act dishonestly, as he might otherwise act in mistake. Finally, *it is to be considered that a close inspection of the standard of precious metal ware is surrounded with very great technical difficulties.* It is, indeed, often impossible, and that not only in the case of very small articles, which would have to be wholly destroyed in order to establish their standard accurately, but also in the case of larger ornaments.

At the sitting of the Committee of the Austrian House of Delegates, on the 16th October, 1863, a person conversant with the subject spoke as follows: " I ask how shall this brooch be brought under control ? It consists of three parts ; the lower rim is hollow, the middle is enamelled, and the upper part is of delicate flowers. Where shall it be inspected, if every part must separately bear a stamp ? Perhaps the pin only is to be subject to control. That will content neither the public nor the authorities ; for every person is at liberty to detach the pin and to fix it on a bad article; in which case I must bear the responsibility." Analogous cases occur very frequently.

It has often happened that chains, necklaces, and bracelets, consisting of several parts, having received the stamp on one part only, have in all the other unstamped parts had gold of a lower standard substituted for the proper one.

Mr. Nessman, Director of the Government offices in Hamburg, who has a thorough practical knowledge of the art of gold manufacture in the provinces, also says: "A teapot of Copenhagen silver being stamped in several places, it was imprudently purchased by me at the worth of Copenhagen silver. When melted down it turned out that the actual body of the teapot—the most considerable part—was of insufficient standard. In the case of chains, the outside parts (terminating links) of which are stamped, even a pretty-well practised eye cannot always detect the lower standard of the parts which are soldered on to them, because the electro-plating gives a similar colour even to the inside parts which cannot be polished."

The public would fare worse, however, if an exact Government control were impossible, and certain categories of precious metal ware were forbidden. The laws collected above contain numerous examples of this; and it is easy to see what great and exceptional hindrances are here laid on a manufacture, and to what an extent the satisfaction of the requirements of luxury is narrowed in this way, and consequently how much more costly the articles become.

So in several states precious metal ware filled with cement, which combined cheapness with the object of the law, is totally forbidden.

The stripe test is insufficient in many cases to establish an accurate investigation ; and even the test in the crucible can only prove the standard of a single portion of an article. To establish accurately the standard of the whole mass of an article of gold or silver it would be required to melt it down. It must be granted that by the increased number of tests adopted the standard may be settled at pleasure. In countries having a preventive State control, the average probability of the standard being decided correctly is not great. Everyone who is interested in this side of the question can easily obtain convincing proof.

Nothing is more significant than the fact, imparted by Mr. Singer, a competent authority, in the Committee of the Austrian Deputies, viz., that the principal testers in Munich, at the time the control was undertaken by the corporation, did not pay respect to the Austrian official control. These gentlemen received knife handles, provided with the official control stamp, in which inferior metal was to be found at the rate of 34 florins' worth in twenty-four handles. Another good authority stated that, in spite of official control, fraud was to be met with "really very frequently, and in much accredited houses or firms."

The "Pforzheim Observer" has over and over again reported cases bearing incontrovertible testimony to the inadequacy of Austrian control. In the issue of that journal for 7th January, 1874, we read that gold rings manufactured in Pforzheim were repeatedly rejected by the Viennese control offices, in spite of their having the legal standard; which shows that business should only be done with Austria with the greatest precaution and care. One cannot shut one's eyes to the fact that the preventive system of control is calculated to injure its business intercourse, even with those foreign nations which are inclined to submit themselves to the restrictions of standard. We hear on all sides, and from many countries, that the imperative-preventive control has not attained its principal object, viz., the protection of the public; and it has therefore been abandoned, as unsatisfactory, in Belgium, Italy, the Swiss Cantons, and elsewhere. Other nations, in the course of their experiments, are arriving at the conclusion that the struggle of competition forms at once the best and the sole security for the protection of the public. Even in France, where the public submit more willingly to State control than in any other country, the system is being shaken; and it may be calculated that the legal limitations to the precious metal trade will at last be remoulded.

If the system of State control for *all* precious metal ware be abolished, it is not of importance that the control should be maintained for a portion of these goods, viz., for wares the manufacturers or sellers of which deem it advisable to add to the reputation of their name the guarantee of the State, or, as not unfrequently happens, to re-establish the former by the help of the latter.

We feel the less inclined to address ourselves to this so-called *facultative* system, which leaves the standard prescribed by imperative-preventive control optional to the seller or manufacturer. For, if the State which *undertook* to watch over the standard of precious metal ware did not succeed in protecting the public from fraud, how shall that State succeed which assumes the control only to oblige? If the State be not in a condition to protect the public from fraud, and yet shelters, with *its credit*, the credit of a certain class of its citizens, it becomes the accomplice of those who endeavour to defraud the public.

Since, however, the system of facultative control has been adopted in several states in which the imperative-preventive control has proved itself untenable, we see on the one hand that the step was too radical in passing at once from preventive control to complete freedom. On the other hand, the influence of the manufacturers to whom this system promises advantage, certainly at the public cost, remains paramount; so it is easy to be understood that, in Geneva, for instance, where the precious metal trade has a great reputation, and finds a large outlet abroad, a decision was made in favour of this system.

There is not the smallest reason why the

same thing should take place in the German empire, for, although the German gold ware is extensively purchased abroad, it really is not on account of its pre-eminent beauty, or special purity of standard, but on account of its cheapness. Cheapness, however, cannot be certified by a government stamp.

The last proposition which we have to examine runs thus:—*To prescribe by law to the manufacturer the marking of the standard and of his own firm, or of a sign for the same.*

This is a proposal which reappears in many of the judgments of the Chambers of Commerce kindly imparted to us.

It is certainly true that this has already taken place in the Grand Duchy of Hesse, through a decree of the 2nd June, 1829, by which the manufacturers of precious metal ware are rendered legally answerable, under penalties, for the correctness of the standard declared; but the question is whether the public will in this way obtain a better protection than the option of a civil lawsuit at present secures to it.

It is next to be considered that responsibility under penalties, in a province where an error may so easily occur, is a vexatious demand upon the manufacturers of precious metal ware; a demand which, in increasing the responsibility in the pursuit of the trade, cannot fail to diminish the number of those who are inclined to devote themselves to it. A rise in the price of precious metal ware must therefore follow upon a law of this nature. The fraudulent dealer, however, will not be deterred by the threat of penal consequences from practising fraud, even to the widest extent. He will consider, with psychological accuracy, that the public, regarding the great risk incurred by every seller of fraudulently announced standards, will never think it worth while, just on that account, to have the ware tested according to its standard. This legislation, therefore, has simply had the effect of throwing the public off its guard. The undoubted increase of fraud is to be foreseen in consequence. These cases of fraud would, however, be less frequently punishable, because, as a rule, they would come to light only on the sale of the object in question at the worth of the metal. But, as articles of precious metal are long preserved, many years would probably have passed by, during which fraudulent persons may have died or disappeared. Even supposing a case of fraud to be for once discovered immediately, how few would there be who would give themselves all the trouble and loss of time involved in going to law. For fraud generally will be practised only upon a buyer who is not likely to have the standard tested; and he, moreover, will be the buyer of ware of small value. The seller will be cautious in the case of a buyer in whose eyes the worth of the metal is of importance.

The remarks we have made are further supported by the fact that the guarantee given to the buyer by a law of this kind is very insufficient. For how small is the worth of a stamp! In the next place, a large group of precious metal ware must of necessity be excluded from stamping; such, for instance, as gold and silver beads, very fine chains, filigree work, and ware covered with enamel. How can a stamp be placed upon these? Thus the legal compulsion of the employers to stamp the manufactured precious metal ware is necessarily subject to a considerable exception.

Again, since it must be left to the judgment of the individual to decide as to ware that will take a stamp and ware that will not, the dishonest dealer will aim at over-passing the limit, and seek to profit by the legally-allowed exceptions, on the pretext of the widest possible sale of wares of a very low standard.

A much larger question is bound up in this of stamping ware manufactured of metal of different standards.

Even the most enthusiastic supporter of the Government regulation of the standard of gold and silver ware, if he have only a suspicion of the exigencies of the trade, will not desire this. What, then, is to be done? In the Committee of the Austrian House of Delegates, to which reference has been made already, a manufacturer showed an ornamental article which would have to receive forty-eight stamps, if all the parts of different standards, and all those parts which could be separated and replaced by others, were to be stamped. How often do such cases occur? How great would be the labour of the manufacturer, for which naturally he would be obliged to reimburse himself; and who would care to buy articles thus covered over with stamps? It has been proposed to prescribe the declaration of the *average* standard. But this can only be found out by melting the article in question. The purchased ware would have to be destroyed that the seller may be under control.

And what is to be done with those articles which consist of precious and of inferior metal, the compound parts of which cannot be separated without destroying the articles? What is the use of the declaration of standard to me if I cannot gauge the quantity of gold or silver in the article? It is, therefore, evident, that in a very large number of cases the proposed law could not be carried out, and that in an equally large number it would be useless.

Even for the remaining cases the stamp does not appear to be advisable. In order that the sign of the manufacturer might assure a proper security, each manufacturer must make use of a separate one; and throughout the German empire every manufacturer would have to deposit his trade-mark in the Imperial Chancellory, whose care it would be to see that every manufacturer had a different one. How easily an exchange might be made is particularly evident from the fact that a maximum size of stamp would require to be prescribed, in order to reduce as much as possible the number of wares which, from their small size, would not bear a stamp. And if a manufacturer were bent on employing a false stamp, consider how easy it is to imitate a stamp; and how difficult in such a case would be the proof! How often have the genuine official stamps been cut out and soldered into wares of lower standard! Can the same thing not be done with a private stamp? How widely, therefore, through the land, would a door and gate be opened for fraud! "As a good father will not disown his children, so the custom of impressing the trade mark of the manufacturer upon machines, lamps, dresses, and so forth, is the sign of a manufacturer confident in the goodness of his wares, and it will be only the false gold manufacturer who will raise objections to this demand (that of stamping his firm and place of abode upon the wares)." So writes Karl Roscher.

We doubt this, most decidedly. It may easily happen that a gold manufacturer of high repute is compelled for a time, at a certain crisis of his affairs, to use a very low standard instead of a high one. It would be of great importance to him to send them out without his stamp, in order that his credit may not suffer; and, if this were not possible, it would be better he should renounce altogether the manufacture of cheap articles.

An author has the liberty of writing anonymously, or with a *nom de plume*, when he is not quite content with his writings; why may not a goldsmith have the same liberty?

Very often it happens that the purchaser himself does not desire the stamps of standard and firm on the article; and the retail dealer not seldom has very great objection to them.

The public, as a rule, are not at all desirous of the firm or the standard being marked on the goods. The bad name of a firm, or a low degree of standard, would make a gift almost worthless. Many who have very little money to spare, and are yet anxious to give pleasure, would be debarred from making any present at all if this were to be insisted upon. And this is a consideration of no small moment in the times in which we live; for it is just in those precious metal wares that are so universally used for presents, and whose principal object is to gratify vanity, that appearance plays the most conspicuous part. Make this impossible, and the German precious metal industry would suffer from the severest blow it could possibly receive.

To demand the stamp of standard on our ware would be simply to brand them in foreign lands.

In the Austrian Chamber of Deputies it was stated "that the Orientals get most of their large supplies from the German manufactories, exactly because they have no stamps upon the wares."

1. The Imperative-preventive Control;
2. The Facultative Control System; and
3. The Manufacturer's Sign or Stamp on the wares, are the three principal systems of legal regulation of the standard of gold and silver ware.

Combinations of these three systems are formed in every conceivable manner; but, as they are formed from the elements which have been under notice, it is not necessary to consider them further. For who cares to make the machinery of the wheel good, when the wheel itself is useless?

PART VII.

WHAT interest have the workers in precious metals and their employers in the question of the legal regulation of exact standards of gold and silver ware?

In Geneva, and the centres of industry—Neufchatel, Jura, in Chaux-de-Fonds and Locll—where the question of the standard was at one time the great question of the day, and swallowed up almost all other interests, many of the working-classes took a very prominent position in battling for the legal regulation of a high standard. In Jura, for instance, the watch-case makers so bestirred themselves. There, as in all centres of precious metal trade, it has been found that the manufacture of gold and silver of high standard leads to a higher average rate of wages than the manufacture of precious metals of a lower standard.

We hear from a Geneva goldsmith—"Generally, handiwork is less remunerated on works of 14 carats than on works of 18 carats."

Naturally! With the increase of value in the raw material the wages of the workmen increase, as they must be of a high class, and able to give security for their trustworthiness and honesty. The manufacturer, therefore, is required to pay a very high price for reliable labour, of which the supply is limited.

Another fact of great importance is, that gold and silver of a high standard are, as a rule, only manufactured into articles whose workmanship is of a high class. Anyone inclined to possess an ornament of greater solid value than usual, will also, to make the outside correspond to the inside, pay a high price for a new and tasteful pattern, beautifully executed. And, that these designs may be skilfully executed, workmen of high class ability are necessary.

The manufacture of precious metal ware of very high standard generally goes hand-in-hand with special care in carrying out the design. But if any design has been multiplied hundreds of times, of course the manufacturer reckons upon purchasers who attach no importance to the possession of new designs, and who are not inclined to spend much money upon gold or silver plate. This class of purchasers, representing the great majority, are, therefore, satisfied with articles made in numbers by machinery, which, as the manufacturer very rightly judges, must, in order to attain their object, be very cheap, and consequently of a low standard.

If, however, it be true that in working high standards the relatively greater trustworthiness and skill of the workman demand a higher rate of wage, still we must not forget that in places where only the manufacture of precious metal of a high standard is allowed by law, the sum total of goods ordered will be correspondingly small, and consequently will only slightly influence the demand for workmen.

Nevertheless, it is also an undoubted fact that the demand for workmen in the manufacture of precious metals of a low standard, having skill and reliability only of a medium order, will be greater than in the other case; and that the collective amount of wages paid will exceed what would have been paid under such a legal restriction. It is not to be doubted that *freedom in the application of the standard tends to the advantage of the workmen.*

If freedom in the choice of the standard tends

to the advantage of the working class, how fares it with the manufacturer?

In relation to this inquiry it must be admitted that in workshops in which ware of a low standard is made, and where customers are proportionately large, the cost of carrying on the business is smaller than in workshops which serve but few customers and employ but few workmen. The rent, the furnishing, and the technical and mercantile superintendence are not, in proportion, as dear in the first as in the last.

Again, the larger manufacturer, who is permitted by law to work all standards, can afford to sell much cheaper ware than one not so favourably situated.

Of course, those who exclusively work at the highest standard will, as a rule, suffer no disadvantage in the event of that alone being legalized.

We must not omit to take into account those periods of stagnation which occur so often and so suddenly in trades specially devoted to luxury. A war, or a crisis in the Funds, operates adversely to them at once. Thus, a Viennese silversmith told us at the Exhihition that he had twenty-three silver dinner-services on hand, with the name and arms of those who had ordered them, owing to some sudden inability on their part to pay for them.

In these times, when trade is so dull, it would be a benefit to many a manufacturer if he could work at what standard he pleased, and so suit the tastes and means of the many. And apart from material gain, he would have the great advantage of being able to retain his staff of skilled workmen, who know the secrets and working of his establishment, instead of dismissing them for lack of employment.

Of course, freedom in the choice of the standard would be an undoubted advantage to the manufacturer.

The Geneva goldsmith above quoted confirms this statement. " Liberty of standard," he says, "is in my opinion a very good thing. If we had it not in Geneva, we should absolutely have nothing to do at this moment."

Let us record here that the goldsmith who writes this generally works only metal of very high standard. His letter is dated April, 1873, a time of serious commercial depression in Geneva.

DEDUCTIONS.

In the foregoing pages it has been shown that experiment and logic alike condemn the legal regulation of the standard of gold and silver ware, and that there is good ground for saying that great advantage would accrue to the public, to the precious metal workers and employers of labour, from freedom in the choice of standard.

The Author submits his opinion that—

Legal regulations for the standard of gold and silver ware do not protect the public against deception; and that they therefore are worthless.

Although we are thoroughly convinced of the correctness of the plan we recommend, we do not conceal from ourselves that, public opinion leaning so strongly towards the advantage of State control, it will be most difficult to effect any change. What has been advanced in the preceding pages abundantly demonstrates the tendency of the precious metal industry towards securing freedom.

The history of the laws and regulations connected with the precious metal industry in those lands where the State has interfered with its course, shows that they are gradually becoming less strict; indeed, in several countries they have been withdrawn, leaving the industry at perfect liberty.

Without undue confidence, we dare express the hope that, notwithstanding the previous decisions of the legislators of Germany on the question of standards, we shall witness the emancipation of the precious metal industry in the German empire.

CONCLUSION.

THE deductions at which Herr Studnitz has arrived — " That legal regulations for the standard of gold and silver ware do not protect the public against deception, and therefore are worthless," will hardly be deemed convincing; for I fear the argument would hold good in favour of abolishing all the machinery for detecting and punishing crime, on the plea that crime still recurs in spite of all our efforts to suppress it.

It seems that the free trade which a dishonest trader would contend for, is that, which ultimately, would make all trade impossible, as it could thrive only so long as the cheat was the pet object of protection.

The allegation that a man of good character may find himself at *a certain crisis* tempted to lower the standard of his gold ware, and then refuse to put his name to the spurious article, for fear his repute should be jeopardized, is not an argument likely to find much favour in a country which has some prejudices left in favour of the policy of honesty.

It is more than possible, that trading on the ignorance or unskilfulness of the public, might lead to a corresponding distrust on their part, not generally credited with the result of raising the profits of trade. Depreciated stock has the knack of falling in the market.

The easy possession of spurious value is a bubble which collapses occasionally.

How the author can sustain the analogy between the *anonymous writer* and the trader, whose good name would be forfeited, were he known to be the issuer of spurious gold ware, is not clear, unless he means that the man who issues the libellous matter, whether with a *nom de plume* or not, is very near the criminal dock. "Why may not a goldsmith have the same liberty?" he asks; I presume he must mean, with the same result.

May I ask, would it not be better for all the trade to work in good faith and in harmony with the Goldsmiths' Company, calling upon that company to resist sternly countenancing in any way the deceptions which are now the subject of severe animadversion from those who advocate the continuance, no less than of those who strive for the abolition, of all marking of gold ware.

It is a reproach to the trade and to the Hall, that nowhere abroad is the public so unprotected against fraud as in England.

I have exhibited publicly a collection of genuine Hall-marked articles, which presented almost every variety of ingenious deception. The Hall-marked gold ware was made so wondrously to personate what they really were not, that the careful purchaser, armed with instructions and using a good magnifying glass, would yet have been deceived. He would have purchased in confidence, and found out the cheat sooner or later.

What ultimate benefit to the trade or to the public would ensue?

If the Goldsmiths' Company will not contribute its influence to remove this scandal, the trade must combine to secure the advantage of a recognised standard for their mutual honour and security, and insist that all articles containing less than 12-carat gold, shall be sold as metal. The standard I should, then, strive to introduce, is that which I have advocated for thirty years, the 18-*carat gold;* the durability and advantages of which my long experience entirely confirms me in persevering to perpetuate.

EDWIN W. STREETER.

18, *New Bond Street, London.*

GOLD.

A View of the Standards of Gold and Silver Wares in different Countries of the World.

COUNTRIES.	STANDARDS.						REMARKS.
	GOLD WARE.				SILVER WARE.		
					oz. dwts.	oz. dwts.	
Great Britain ...	24	22	18	15 12 9	11 10	11 2	No Laws.
Her Colonies ...				...	...	...	No special Laws.
United States ...				...	...	...	
States of S. America							
France		$\frac{840}{1000}$		$\frac{750}{1000}$	$\frac{950}{1000}$	$\frac{800}{1000}$	Lower than this is for export only.
Denmark				$\frac{750}{1000}$			No special Laws.
Turkey				$\frac{750}{1000}$	$\frac{900}{1000}$		
Greece				...	...	...	No Laws.
Belgium				$\frac{750}{1000}$	$\frac{900}{1000}$	$\frac{800}{1000}$	Not compulsory.
Holland	$\frac{916}{1000}$	$\frac{833}{1000}$		$\frac{750}{1000}$ $\frac{583}{1000}$	$\frac{934}{1000}$	$\frac{800}{1000}$	Not compulsory.
Italy	$\frac{900}{1000}$			$\frac{750}{1000}$ $\frac{800}{1000}$	$\frac{950}{1000}$	$\frac{800}{1000}$	
Spain	$\frac{916}{1000}$			$\frac{833}{1000}$ $\frac{750}{1000}$	$\frac{916}{1000}$	$\frac{750}{1000}$	
Portugal				$\frac{840\frac{1}{2}}{1000}$	$\frac{843\frac{1}{2}}{1000}$		
Austria	$\frac{930}{1000}$	$\frac{840}{1000}$		$\frac{750}{1000}$ $\frac{580}{1000}$	$\frac{950}{1000}$ $\frac{800}{1000}$	$\frac{750}{1000}$	

GOLD.

COUNTRIES.	STANDARDS.		REMARKS.
	GOLD WARE.	SILVER WARE.	
Russia ...	$\frac{583}{1000}$ $\frac{750}{1000}$ $\frac{850}{1000}$	$\frac{847\frac{1}{2}}{1000}$	
Basle ...	$\frac{750}{1000}$	$\frac{787}{1000}$	Not compulsory.
Geneva ...	$\frac{750}{1000}$	$\frac{800}{1000}$	
Glarus ...	...	$\frac{750}{1000}$	
Lucerne ...	$\frac{750}{1000}$		
Neufchatel ...	$\frac{583}{1000}$	$\frac{800}{1000}$	Not compulsory.
Pays de Vaud...	$\frac{750}{1000}$	$\frac{800}{1000}$	Not compulsory.
Brazil ...	$\frac{750}{1000}$		
Sax Meiningen*	...		
Sweden ...	$\frac{975\frac{3}{4}}{1000}$ $\frac{847\frac{3}{4}}{1000}$ $\frac{793\frac{3}{4}}{1000}$	$\frac{750}{1000}$ $\frac{816\frac{3}{4}}{1000}$ $\frac{830\frac{1}{4}}{1000}$	
Norway ...	$\frac{750}{1000}$ $\frac{583}{1000}$ $\frac{750}{1000}$	$\frac{800}{1000}$	
Alsace and Lorraine	$\frac{920}{1000}$ $\frac{840}{1000}$	$\frac{950}{1000}$	
Oldenburg ...	...	$\frac{750}{1000}$	
Altenburg ...	...	$\frac{750}{1000}$	
Hamburg...	...	$\frac{721}{1000}$	
Egypt ...	$\frac{750}{1000}$	...	Same as Turkey.
Morocco ...	$\frac{1000}{1000}$	...	Same as France.
China ...	$\frac{725}{1000}$ $\frac{750}{1000}$	...	Quite pure.
Persia ...	$\frac{795}{1000}$		No special Laws.
Japan ...	$\frac{958\frac{1}{3}}{1000}$		

As in nearly all Countries of the World the Standards are expressed in 1000ths, we give the following Table.

$\frac{41\frac{2}{3}}{1000}$	equal	1	carat	$\frac{541\frac{2}{3}}{1000}$	equal	13	carats
$\frac{83\frac{1}{3}}{1000}$	„	2	„	$\frac{583\frac{1}{3}}{1000}$	„	14	„
$\frac{125}{1000}$	„	3	„	$\frac{625}{1000}$	„	15	„
$\frac{166\frac{2}{3}}{1000}$	„	4	„	$\frac{666\frac{2}{3}}{1000}$	„	16	„
$\frac{208\frac{1}{3}}{1000}$	„	5	„	$\frac{708\frac{1}{3}}{1000}$	„	17	„
$\frac{250}{1000}$	„	6	„	$\frac{750}{1000}$	„	18	„
$\frac{291\frac{2}{3}}{1000}$	„	7	„	$\frac{791\frac{2}{3}}{1000}$	„	19	„
$\frac{333\frac{1}{3}}{1000}$	„	8	„	$\frac{833\frac{1}{3}}{1000}$	„	20	„
$\frac{375}{1000}$	„	9	„	$\frac{875}{1000}$	„	21	„
$\frac{416\frac{2}{3}}{1000}$	„	10	„	$\frac{916\frac{2}{3}}{1000}$	„	22	„
$\frac{458\frac{1}{3}}{1000}$	„	11	„	$\frac{958\frac{1}{3}}{1000}$	„	23	„
$\frac{500}{1000}$	„	12	„	$\frac{1000}{1000}$	„	24	„

Table showing the value per ounce of the different qualities of Gold, calculated at the highest Mint prices.

Gold of		Worth per ounce.			Gold of		Worth per ounce.		
Car.	Grs.	£	s.	d.	Car.	Grs.	£	s.	d.
24	0	4	4	11½	20	1	3	11	8¼
23	3	4	4	0¾	20	0	3	10	9½
23	2	4	3	2¼	19	3	3	9	11
23	1	4	2	3½	19	2	3	9	0¼
23	0	4	1	5	19	1	3	8	1¾
22	3	4	0	6¼	19	0	3	7	3
22	2	3	19	7¾	18	3	3	6	4½
22	1	3	18	9	18	2	3	5	5¾
22	0	3	17	10½	18	1	3	4	7¼
21	3	3	16	11¾	18	0	3	3	8½
21	2	3	16	1¼	17	3	3	2	10
21	1	3	15	2½	17	2	3	1	11¼
21	0	3	14	4	17	1	3	1	0¾
20	3	3	13	5½	17	0	3	0	2
20	2	3	12	6¾	16	3	2	19	3½

GOLD.

Table showing the value per ounce of the different qualities of Gold, calculated at the highest Mint prices.

GOLD of		Worth per ounce.			GOLD of		Worth per ounce.		
Car.	Grs.	£	s.	d.	Car.	Grs.	£	s.	d.
16	2	2	18	4¾	8	1	1	9	2½
16	1	2	17	6¼	8	0	1	8	3¾
16	0	2	16	7¾	7	3	1	7	5¼
15	3	2	15	9	7	2	1	6	6½
15	2	2	14	10¼	7	1	1	5	8
15	1	2	13	11¾	7	0	1	4	9¼
15	0	2	13	1	6	3	1	3	10¾
14	3	2	12	2½	6	2	1	3	0
14	2	2	11	4	6	1	1	2	1½
14	1	2	10	5¼	6	0	1	1	2¼
14	0	2	9	6¾	5	3	1	0	4¼
13	3	2	8	8	5	2	0	19	5½
13	2	2	7	9½	5	1	0	18	7
13	1	2	6	10¾	5	0	0	17	8¼
13	0	2	6	0¼	4	3	0	16	9¾
12	3	2	5	1½	4	2	0	15	11¼
12	2	2	4	3	4	1	0	15	0½
12	1	2	3	4¼	4	0	0	14	2
12	0	2	2	5¾	3	3	0	13	3¼
11	3	2	1	7	3	2	0	12	4¾
11	2	2	0	8½	3	1	0	11	6
11	1	1	19	9¾	3	0	0	10	7½
11	0	1	18	11¼	2	3	0	9	8¾
10	3	1	18	0½	2	2	0	8	10¼
10	2	1	17	2	2	1	0	7	11½
10	1	1	16	3½	2	0	0	7	1
10	0	1	15	4¾	1	3	0	6	2¼
9	3	1	14	6¼	1	2	0	5	3¾
9	2	1	13	7½	1	1	0	4	5
9	1	1	12	9	1	0	0	3	6½
9	0	1	11	10½	0	3	0	2	7¾
8	3	1	10	11¾	0	2	0	1	9¼
8	2	1	10	1	0	1	0	0	10½

ERRATA.

Page xvi., line 10 from top, for Βάνανορ, read Βάσανο
Page 21, line 11 from top, for *Millaner*, read *Millauer*.
Page 21, line 19 from top, for Iliero, read Hiero.
Page 66, line 15 from top, for Moonsickle, read Crescent.

October, 1876.

CHATTO & WINDUS'S
LIST OF BOOKS.

NEW FINE-ART GIFT-BOOK, UNIFORM WITH THE
"TURNER GALLERY."

Handsomely half-bound, India Proofs, royal folio, £10 ; Large Paper copies, Artists' India Proofs, elephant folio, £20.

Modern Art:

A Series of superb Line Engravings, from the Works of distinguished Painters of the English and Foreign Schools, selected from Galleries and Private Collections in Great Britain.

With Descriptive Text by JAMES DAFFORNE.

Demy 8vo, price One Shilling.

Academy Notes for 1876.

With 107 Illustrations of the Principal Pictures at Burlington House : a large number being Facsimiles of Sketches drawn by the Artists. Edited by HENRY BLACKBURN.

" *We at once take an opportunity of offering our thanks, as well as those of all visitors to the Exhibition, to Mr. Blackburn for his very carefully executed review of the Academy pictures, illustrated by some 100 woodcut memoranda of the principal pictures, almost half of them from the pencils of the painters themselves. A cheaper, prettier, or more convenient souvenir of the Exhibition it would be difficult to conceive and unreasonable to expect.*"—TIMES.

*** ACADEMY NOTES *for* 1875 *may also be had, price One Shilling.*

BOOKS PUBLISHED BY

Crown 8vo, with Coloured Frontispiece and Illustrations, cloth gilt, 7s. 6d.

A History of Advertising.

From the Earliest Times. Illustrated by Anecdotes, Curious Specimens, and Biographical Notes of Successful Advertisers. By HENRY SAMPSON.

"*We have here a book to be thankful for. Among the many interesting illustrations is a photographed copy of the 'Times' for January 1st, 1788, which may be easily read by means of a magnifying glass. We recommend the present volume, which takes us through antiquity, the Middle Ages, and the present time, illustrating all in turn by advertisements—serious, comic, roguish, or downright rascally. The chapter on 'swindles and hoaxes' is full of entertainment; but of that the volume itself is full from the first page to the last.*"—ATHENÆUM.

Crown 4to, containing 24 Plates beautifully printed in Colours, with descriptive Text, cloth extra, gilt, 6s.

Æsop's Fables

Translated into Human Nature. By C. H. BENNETT.

"*For fun and frolic the new version of Æsop's Fables must bear away the palm. There are plenty of grown-up children who like to be amused; and if this new version of old stories does not amuse them they must be very dull indeed, and their situation one much to be commiserated.*"—MORNING POST.

Crown 8vo, with Portrait and Facsimile, cloth extra, 7s. 6d.

Artemus Ward's Works:

The Works of CHARLES FARRER BROWNE, better known as ARTEMUS WARD. With Portrait, facsimile of Handwriting, &c.

"*The author combines the powers of Thackeray with those of Albert Smith. The salt is rubbed in with a native hand—one which has the gift of tickling.*"—SATURDAY REVIEW.

Small 4to, green and gold, 6s. 6d.; gilt edges, 7s. 6d.

As Pretty as Seven,

and other Popular German Stories. Collected by LUDWIG BECHSTEIN. With Additional Tales by the Brothers GRIMM, and 100 Illustrations by RICHTER.

"*These tales are pure and healthful; they will shed over childhood a rosy light, and strew the path with stars and flowers, the remembrance of which will last through life.*"—PREFACE.

Blake's Works.

A Series of Reproductions in Facsimile of the Works of WILLIAM BLAKE, including the "Songs of Innocence and Experience," "The Book of Thel," "America," "The Vision of the Daughters of Albion," "The Marriage of Heaven and Hell," "Europe, a Prophecy," "Jerusalem," "Milton," "Urizen," "The Song of Los," &c., is now in preparation.

Demy 8vo, cloth extra, with Illustrations, 18s.
Baker's Clouds in the East:
Travels and Adventures on the Perso-Turkoman Frontier. By VALENTINE BAKER. With Maps and Illustrations, coloured and plain, from Original Sketches. Second Edition, revised and corrected.

"*A man who not only thinks for himself, but who has risked his life in order to gain information. . . . . A most graphic and lively narrative of travels and adventures which have nothing of the commonplace about them.*"—LEEDS MERCURY.

Crown 8vo, cloth extra, 7s. 6d.
A Handbook of London Bankers;
With some Account of their Predecessors, the Early Goldsmiths; together with Lists of Bankers, from the Earliest London Directory, printed in 1677, to that of the London Post-Office Directory of 1876. By F. G. HILTON PRICE.

"*An interesting and unpretending little work, which may prove a useful contribution towards the history of a difficult subject. . . . Mr. Price's anecdotes are entertaining. . . . There is something fascinating, almost romantic, in the details given us of Child's Bank. . . . There is a great deal of amusing reading and some valuable information in this book.*"—SATURDAY REVIEW.

"*A work of considerable research and labour; an instructive contribution to the history of the enormous wealth of the City of London.*"—ACADEMY.

Crown 8vo, cloth extra, 9s.
Bardsley's Our English Surnames:
Their Sources and Significations. By CHARLES WAREING BARDSLEY, M.A. Second Edition, revised throughout, considerably enlarged, and partially rewritten.

"*Mr. Bardsley has faithfully consulted the original mediæval documents and works from which the origin and development of surnames can alone be satisfactorily traced. He has furnished a valuable contribution to the literature of surnames, and we hope to hear more of him in this field.*"—TIMES.

Small 8vo, cloth extra, 7s. 6d.
Blewitt's The Rose and the Lily:
How they became the Emblems of England and France. A Fairy Tale. By Mrs. OCTAVIAN BLEWITT. With a Frontispiece by GEORGE CRUIKSHANK.

Crown 8vo, cloth extra gilt, with Illustrations, 7s. 6d.
Boccaccio's Decameron;
or, Ten Days' Entertainment. Translated into English, with an Introduction by THOMAS WRIGHT, Esq., M.A., F.S.A. With Portrait, and STOTHARD's beautiful Copperplates.

BOOKS PUBLISHED BY

Imperial 4to, cloth extra, gilt and gilt edges, price 21s. per volume.

Beautiful Pictures by British Artists:

A Gathering of Favourites from our Picture Galleries. In Two Series.

The FIRST SERIES including Examples by WILKIE, CONSTABLE, TURNER, MULREADY, LANDSEER, MACLISE, E. M. WARD, FRITH, Sir JOHN GILBERT, LESLIE, ANSDELL, MARCUS STONE, Sir NOEL PATON, FAED, EYRE CROWE, GAVIN O'NEIL, and MADOX BROWN.

The SECOND SERIES containing Pictures by ARMYTAGE, FAED, GOODALL, HEMSLEY, HORSLEY, MARKS, NICHOLLS, Sir NOEL PATON, PICKERSGILL, G. SMITH, MARCUS STONE, SOLOMON, STRAIGHT, E. M. WARD, and WARREN.

All engraved on Steel in the highest style of Art. Edited, with Notices of the Artists, by SYDNEY ARMYTAGE, M.A.

Each Volume is Complete in itself.

"*This book is well got up, and good engravings by Jeens, Lumb Stocks, and others, bring back to us pictures of Royal Academy Exhibitions of past years.*"
—TIMES.

Price One Shilling Monthly, with Four Illustrations.

Belgravia.

CONTENTS OF THE OCTOBER NUMBER.

Reality. By CHARLES READE. Illustrated.
Beau Feilding at the Old Bailey. By G. A. SALA.
Juliet. By Mrs. LOVETT CAMERON. Illustrated.
Black Rupert's Leap. Illustrated.
The New Republic.
From Dreams to Waking. By E. LYNN LINTON.
Cupid's Alley. By AUSTIN DOBSON.
Tasbrook's Testimonial. By JAMES PAYN.
Joshua Haggard's Daughter. By M. E. BRADDON. Illustrated.

The THIRTIETH *Volume of* BELGRAVIA (*which includes the* HOLIDAY NUMBER), *elegantly bound in crimson cloth, bevelled boards, full gilt side and back, gilt edges, price* 7s. 6d., *is now ready.—Cases for binding the volume* (*designed by Luke Limner*) *can also be had, price* 2s. 6d. *each.*

On November 10 will be published, price One Shilling, with numerous Illustrations,

The Belgravia Annual

for Christmas, 1876. Containing Stories by GEORGE AUGUSTUS SALA, DUTTON COOK, M. E. BRADDON, MARY CECIL HAY, KATHARINE S. MACQUOID, JAMES PAYN, S. J. MACKENNA, J. S. SULLIVAN, and others.

Crown 8vo, with Photographic Portrait, cloth extra, 9s.

Blanchard's (Laman) Poems.

Now first Collected. Edited, with a Life of the Author (including numerous hitherto unpublished Letters from Lord LYTTON, LAMB, DICKENS, ROBERT BROWNING, and others), by BLANCHARD JERROLD.

"*His humorous verse is much of it admirable—sparkling with genuine 'esprit,' and as polished and pointed as Praed's.*"—SCOTSMAN.

Crown 8vo, cloth extra, gilt, 6s.

Boudoir Ballads:

Vers de Société. By J. ASHBY-STERRY.

Crown 8vo, cloth extra, gilt, 7s. 6d.

Brand's Observations on Popular Antiquities,

chiefly Illustrating the Origin of our Vulgar Customs, Ceremonies, and Superstitions. With the Additions of Sir HENRY ELLIS. An entirely New and Revised Edition, with fine full-page Illustrations.

"*Anyone who will read, on each respective day, the chapter which belongs to it, will, when he has got through the volume, have a better notion of what English history is than he will get from almost any other work professedly named a 'history.'*"—QUARTERLY REVIEW.

Crown 8vo, cloth extra, 7s. 6d.

Bret Harte's Select Works

in Prose and Poetry. With Introductory Essay by J. M. BELLEW, Portrait of the Author, and 50 Illustrations.

"*Not many months before my friend's death, he had sent me two sketches by a young American writer (Bret Harte), far away in California ('The Outcasts of Poker Flat,' and another), in which he had found such subtle strokes of character as he had not anywhere else in late years discovered; the manner resembling himself, but the matter fresh to a degree that had surprised him; the painting in all respects masterly, and the wild rude thing painted a quite wonderful reality. I have rarely known him more honestly moved.*"—FORSTER'S LIFE OF DICKENS.

Small crown 8vo, cloth extra, gilt, with full-page Portraits, 4s. 6d.

Brewster's (Sir David) Martyrs of Science.

Small crown 8vo, cloth extra, gilt, with Astronomical Plates, 4s. 6d.

Brewster's (Sir David) More Worlds

than One, the Creed of the Philosopher and the Hope of the Christian.

Crown 8vo, cloth, full gilt (from a special and novel design), 10s. 6d.

The Bric-a-Brac Hunter;

or, Chapters on Chinamania. By Major H. BYNG HALL. With Photographic Frontispiece.

"*This is a delightful book. His hints respecting marks, texture, finish, and character of various wares will be useful to amateurs. By all who are interested in Chinamania it will be most warmly appreciated—a very amusing and chatty volume.*"—STANDARD.

Small crown 8vo, cloth extra, 6s.

Brillat-Savarin's Gastronomy as a Fine

Art; or, The Science of Good Living. A Translation of the "Physiologie du Goût" of BRILLAT-SAVARIN, with an Introduction and Explanatory Notes by R. E. ANDERSON, M.A.

"*I could write a better book of cookery than has ever yet been written; it should be a book on philosophical principles.*"—Dr. JOHNSON.

THE STOTHARD BUNYAN.—Crown 8vo, cloth extra, gilt, 7s. 6d.

Bunyan's Pilgrim's Progress.

Edited by Rev. T. SCOTT. With 17 beautiful Steel Plates by STOTHARD, engraved by GOODALL; and numerous Woodcuts.

Crown 8vo, cloth extra, gilt, with Illustrations, 7s. 6d.

Byron's Letters and Journals.

With Notices of his Life. By THOMAS MOORE. A Reprint of the Original Edition, newly revised, Complete in one thick Volume, with Twelve full-page Plates.

"*We have read this book with the greatest pleasure. Considered merely as a composition, it deserves to be classed among the best specimens of English prose which our age has produced. . . . The style is agreeable, clear, and manly, and, when it rises into eloquence, it rises without effort or ostentation. Nor is the matter inferior to the manner. It would be difficult to name a book which exhibits more kindness, fairness, and modesty.*"—MACAULAY.

Demy 4to, cloth extra, gilt edges, 31s. 6d.

Canova's Works in Sculpture and Modelling.

150 Plates, exquisitely engraved in Outline by MOSES, and printed on an India tint. With Descriptions by the Countess ALBRIZZI, a Biographical Memoir by CICOGNARA, and Portrait by WORTHINGTON.

"*The fertility of this master's resources is amazing, and the manual labour expended on his works would have worn out many an ordinary workman. The outline engravings are finely executed. The descriptive notes are discriminating, and in the main exact.*"—SPECTATOR.

"*A very handsome volume. . . . The graceful designs of the original are rendered by the engraver with exquisite fidelity. As a gift-book, the volume deserves to be placed beside the 'Outlines' of a very kindred genius—Flaxman.*"—GRAPHIC.

Two Vols. imperial 8vo, cloth extra, gilt, the Plates beautifully
printed in Colours, £3 3s.

Catlin's Illustrations of the Manners,
Customs, and Condition of the North American Indians: the result of Eight Years of Travel and Adventure among the Wildest and most Remarkable Tribes now existing. Containing 360 Coloured Engravings from the Author's original Paintings.

Imperial folio, half-morocco, gilt, £7 10s.

Catlin's North American Indian Portfolio.
Containing Hunting Scenes, Amusements, Scenery, and Costume of the Indians of the Rocky Mountains and Prairies of America, from Drawings and Notes made by the Author during Eight Years' Travel. A series of 31 magnificent Plates, beautifully coloured in facsimile of the Original Drawings exhibited at the Egyptian Hall.

Crown 8vo, cloth extra, gilt, 7s. 6d.

Colman's Humorous Works:
"Broad Grins," "My Nightgown and Slippers," and other Humorous Works, Prose and Poetical, of GEORGE COLMAN. With Life and Anecdotes by G. B. BUCKSTONE, and Frontispiece by HOGARTH.

"*What antic have we here, in motley livery of red and yellow, with cap on head, and dagger of lath in hand? It is the king's jester, a professed droll, strangely gifted in all grimace, who pulls faces, and sells grins by the yard. For the impudent joke he has scarcely an equal.*"—WESTMINSTER REVIEW.

Demy 8vo, cloth extra, with Coloured Illustrations and Maps, 21s.

Cope's History of the Rifle Brigade
(The Prince Consort's Own), formerly the 95th. By Sir WILLIAM H. COPE, formerly Lieutenant Rifle Brigade.

Crown 8vo, cloth extra, gilt, with Portraits, 7s. 6d.

Creasy's Memoirs of Eminent Etonians;
with Notices of the Early History of Eton College. By Sir EDWARD CREASY, Author of "The Fifteen Decisive Battles of the World." A New Edition, brought down to the Present Time, with 13 Illustrations.

"*A new edition of 'Creasy's Etonians' will be welcome. The book was a favourite a quarter of a century ago, and it has maintained its reputation. The value of this new edition is enhanced by the fact that Sir Edward Creasy has added to it several memoirs of Etonians who have died since the first edition appeared. The work is eminently interesting.*"—SCOTSMAN.

Crown 8vo, cloth gilt, Two very thick Volumes, 7s. 6d. each.

Cruikshank's Comic Almanack.

Complete in Two SERIES: The FIRST from 1835 to 1843; the SECOND from 1844 to 1853. A Gathering of the BEST HUMOUR of THACKERAY, HOOD, MAYHEW, ALBERT SMITH, A'BECKETT, ROBERT BROUGH, &c. With 2000 Woodcuts and Steel Engravings by CRUIKSHANK, HINE, LANDELLS, &c.

To be Completed in Twenty-four Parts, quarto, at Five Shillings each, profusely illustrated by Coloured and Plain Plates and Wood Engravings,

The Cyclopædia of Costume;

or, A Dictionary of Dress—Regal, Ecclesiastical, Civil and Military—from the Earliest Period in England to the reign of George the Third. Including Notices of Contemporaneous Fashions on the Continent, and preceded by a General History of the Costumes of the Principal Countries of Europe. By J. R. PLANCHÉ, Somerset Herald.—A Prospectus will be sent upon application. Part XV. just ready.

"*There is no subject connected with dress with which 'Somerset Herald' is not as familiar as ordinary men are with the ordinary themes of everyday life. The gathered knowledge of many years is placed before the world in this his latest work, and, when finished, there will exist no work on the subject half so valuable. The numerous illustrations are all effective—for their accuracy the author is responsible; they are well drawn and well engraved, and, while indispensable to a proper comprehension of the text, are satisfactory as works of art.*"—ART JOURNAL.

"*One of the most perfect works ever published upon the subject. . . . Beautifully printed and superbly illustrated.*"—STANDARD.

*** *Part XIV. contains the Completion of the DICTIONARY, which, as Vol. I. of the Book, forms a Complete Work in itself. This volume may now be had, handsomely bound in half red morocco, gilt top, price £3 13s. 6d. Cases for binding the volume may also be had, price 5s. each.*

The remaining Parts will be occupied by the GENERAL HISTORY OF THE COSTUMES OF EUROPE, arranged Chronologically.

Crown 8vo, cloth extra, gilt and emblazoned, with Illustrations, coloured and plain, 7s. 6d.

Cussans' Handbook of Heraldry.

With Instructions for Tracing Pedigrees and Deciphering Ancient MSS.; Rules for the Appointment of Liveries, Chapters on Continental and American Heraldry, &c. &c. By JOHN E. CUSSANS. Illustrated with 360 Plates and Woodcuts.

Parts I. to X. now ready, 21s. each.

Cussans' History of Hertfordshire.

A County History, got up in a very superior manner, and ranging with the finest works of its class. By JOHN E. CUSSANS. Illustrated with full-page Plates on Copper and Stone, and a profusion of small Woodcuts.

"*Mr. Cussans has, from sources not accessible to Clutterbuck, made most valuable additions to the manorial history of the county, from the earliest period downwards, cleared up many doubtful points, and given original details concerning various subjects untouched or imperfectly treated by that writer. The same may be said as to the lists of incumbents and the monumental inscriptions. Clutterbuck's errors and omissions have been carefully corrected and supplied, and the occurrences of the last fifty years added, so that we have these important features of the work complete. Particular attention has also been paid to the heraldry of the county. . . . The pedigrees seem to have been constructed with great care, and are a valuable addition to the genealogical history of the county. Mr. Cussans appears to have done his work conscientiously, and to have spared neither time, labour, nor expense to render his volumes worthy of ranking in the highest class of County Histories. The typography is entitled to unqualified praise, the paper, type, and illustrations being unexceptionable.*"—ACADEMY.

Demy 8vo, half-bound morocco, 21s.

Dibdin's Bibliomania;

or, Book-Madness: A Bibliographical Romance. With numerous Illustrations. A New Edition, with a Supplement, including a Key to the Assumed Characters in the Drama.

"*I have not yet recovered from the delightful delirium into which your 'Bibliomania' has completely thrown me. Your book, to my taste, is one of the most extraordinary gratifications I have enjoyed for many years.*"—ISAAC DISRAELI.

Two Vols., 8vo, cloth extra, 30s.

Dixon's White Conquest:

America in 1875. By W. HEPWORTH DIXON.

"*The best written, most instructive, and most entertaining book that Mr. Dixon has published since 'New America.'*"—ATHENÆUM.

SECOND EDITION, demy 8vo, cloth gilt, with Illustrations, 18s.

Dunraven's The Great Divide:

A Narrative of Travels in the Upper Yellowstone in the summer of 1874. By the EARL of DUNRAVEN. With Maps and numerous striking full-page Illustrations by VALENTINE W. BROMLEY.

"*There has not for a long time appeared a better book of travel than Lord Dunraven's 'The Great Divide.' . . . The book is full of clever observation, and both narrative and illustrations are thoroughly good.*"—ATHENÆUM.

"*A jolly, rollicking narrative of adventure and sport, mixed up with a great deal of useful information concerning one of the most interesting regions in the American continent.*"—NATURE.

Demy 8vo, cloth extra, with Illustrations, 24s.

Dodge's (Colonel) The Hunting Grounds

of the Great West: a Description of the Plains, Game, and Indians of the Great North American Desert. By RICHARD IRVING DODGE, Lieutenant-Colonel of the United States Army. With an Introduction by WILLIAM BLACKMORE; Map, and numerous Illustrations drawn by ERNEST GRISET.

Crown 8vo, cloth boards, 6s. per Volume ; a few Large Paper copies (only 50 printed), at 12s. per Vol.

Early English Poets.

Edited, with Introductions and Annotations, by the Rev. A. B. GROSART.

"*Mr. Grosart has spent the most laborious and the most enthusiastic care on the perfect restoration and preservation of the text; and it is very unlikely that any other edition of the poet can ever be called for. . . From Mr. Grosart we always expect and always receive the final results of most patient and competent scholarship.*"—EXAMINER.

1. *Fletcher's (Giles, B.D.)* Complete Poems: Christ's Victorie in Heaven, Christ's Victorie on Earth, Christ's Triumph over Death, and Minor Poems. With Memorial-Introduction and Notes.

2. *Davies' (Sir John)* Complete Poetical Works, including Psalms I. to L. in Verse, and other hitherto Unpublished MSS., for the first time Collected and Edited. With Memorial-Introduction and Notes. Two Vols.

3. *Herrick's (Robert) Hesperides, Noble Numbers, and* Complete Collected Poems. With Memorial-Introduction and Notes, Steel Portrait, Index of First Lines, and Glossarial Index, &c. Three Vols.

4. *Sidney's (Sir Philip)* Complete Poetical Works, including all those in "Arcadia." With Memorial-Introduction, Essay on the Poetry of Sidney, and Notes. [*In the press.*

5. *Donne's (Dr. John)* Complete Poetical Works, including the Satires and various from MSS. With Memorial-Introduction and Notes. [*In the press.*

*** *Other volumes are in active preparation.*

Crown 8vo, cloth extra, gilt, with Illustrations, 6s.

Emanuel On Diamonds and Precious

Stones: their History, Value, and Properties ; with Simple Tests for ascertaining their Reality. By HARRY EMANUEL, F.R.G.S. With numerous Illustrations, Tinted and Plain.

Crown 8vo, cloth extra, with Illustrations, 7s. 6d.

The Englishman's House:

A Practical Guide to all interested in Selecting or Building a House, with full Estimates of Cost, Quantities, &c. By C. J. RICHARDSON. Third Edition. With nearly 600 Illustrations.

Crown 8vo, cloth extra, with Illustrations, 6s.

Fairholt's Tobacco:

Its History and Associations; including an Account of the Plant and its Manufacture; with its Modes of Use in all Ages and Countries. By F. W. FAIRHOLT, F.S.A. A New Edition, with Coloured Frontispiece and upwards of 100 Illustrations by the Author.

"*A very pleasant and instructive history of tobacco and its associations, which we cordially recommend alike to the votaries and to the enemies of the much-maligned but certainly not neglected weed. . . . Full of interest and information.*"—DAILY NEWS.

"*A more complete and dainty book on a subject which some still think unsavoury it would not be easy to call to mind.*"—GRAPHIC.

Crown 8vo, cloth extra, with Illustrations, 4s. 6d.

Faraday's Chemical History of a Candle.

Lectures delivered to a Juvenile Audience. A New Edition. Edited by W. CROOKES, F.C.S. With numerous Illustrations.

Crown 8vo, cloth extra, with Illustrations, 4s. 6d.

Faraday's Various Forces of Nature.

A New Edition. Edited by W. CROOKES, F.C.S. With numerous Illustrations.

Crown 8vo, cloth extra, with Illustrations, 7s. 6d.

Finger-Ring Lore:

Historical, Legendary, and Anecdotal.—Earliest Notices; Superstitions; Ring Investiture, Secular and Ecclesiastical; Betrothal and Wedding Rings; Ring-tokens; Memorial and Mortuary Rings; Posy-Rings; Customs and Incidents in Connection with Rings; Remarkable Rings, &c. By WILLIAM JONES, F.S.A. With Hundreds of Illustrations of Curious Rings of all Ages and Countries.

"*The book is both amusing and instructive.*"—DAILY TELEGRAPH.

"*Enters fully into the whole subject, and gives an amount of information and general reading in reference thereto which is of very high interest. The book is not only a sort of history of finger-rings, but is a collection of anecdotes in connection with them. . . . The volume is admirably illustrated, and altogether affords an amount of amusement and information which is not otherwise easily accessible.*"—SCOTSMAN.

"*One of those gossiping books which are as full of amusement as of instruction.*"—ATHENÆUM.

Demy 8vo, cloth extra, gilt, with Illustrations, 9s.
Figuier's Primitive Man:
A Popular Manual of the prevailing Theories of the Descent of Man, as promulgated by DARWIN, LYELL, Sir JOHN LUBBOCK, HUXLEY, E. B. TYLOR, and other eminent Ethnologists. Translated from the last French edition, and revised by E. B. T. With 263 Illustrations.

"*An interesting and essentially popular résumé of all that has been written on the subject. M. Figuier has collected together the evidences which modern researches have accumulated, and has done this with a considerable amount of care.*"—ATHENÆUM.

Demy 8vo, cloth extra, with Illustrations, 18s.
Gay's From Pall Mall to the Punjaub;
or, With the Prince in India. By J. DREW GAY. With fine full-page Illustrations.

"*A lasting memorial of an interesting journey.*"—DAILY TELEGRAPH.
"*Written in a lively and unpretentious style, and sparkling here and there with genuine humour, the work is a decidedly attractive one.*"—LEEDS MERCURY.
"*A very readable and enjoyable narrative of a journey whose importance and interest are already part of history.*"—HOME NEWS.

Demy 8vo, cloth extra, gilt, with Illustrations, 18s.
Gell and Gandy's Pompeiana;
or, The Topography, Edifices, and Ornaments of Pompeii. With upwards of 100 Line Engravings by GOODALL, COOKE, HEATH, PYE, &c.

THE RUSKIN GRIMM.—Square crown 8vo, cloth extra, 6s. 6d.; gilt edges, 7s. 6d.
German Popular Stories.
Collected by the Brothers GRIMM, and Translated by EDGAR TAYLOR. Edited, with an Introduction, by JOHN RUSKIN. With 22 Illustrations after the inimitable designs of GEORGE CRUIKSHANK. Both Series Complete.

"*The illustrations of this volume . . . . are of quite sterling and admirable art, of a class precisely parallel in elevation to the character of the tales which they illustrate; and the original etchings, as I have before said in the Appendix to my 'Elements of Drawing,' were unrivalled in masterfulness of touch since Rembrandt (in some qualities of delineation, unrivalled even by him). . . . To make somewhat enlarged copies of them, looking at them through a magnifying glass, and never putting two lines where Cruikshank has put only one, would be an exercise in decision and severe drawing which would leave afterwards little to be learnt in schools.*"—*Extract from Introduction by* JOHN RUSKIN.

One Vol. crown 8vo, cloth extra, 9s.
Gilbert's (W. S.) Original Plays:
"A Wicked World," "Charity," "The Palace of Truth," "Pygmalion," "Trial by Jury," &c.

"*His workmanship is in its way perfect; it is very sound, very even, very well sustained, and excellently balanced throughout.*"—OBSERVER.

Demy 4to, cloth extra, with Illustrations, 31s. 6d.
Gillray the Caricaturist:
The Story of his Life and Times, with Anecdotal Descriptions of his Engravings. Edited by THOMAS WRIGHT, Esq., M.A., F.S.A. With 83 full-page Plates, and numerous Wood Engravings.

"*High as the expectations excited by this description [in the Introduction] may be, they will not be disappointed. The most inquisitive or exacting reader will find ready gathered to his hand, without the trouble of reference, almost every scrap of narrative, anecdote, gossip, scandal, or epigram, that he can possibly require for the elucidation of the caricatures.*"—QUARTERLY REVIEW.

Crown 8vo, cloth extra, with a Map, 3s. 6d.
Gold;
Or, Legal Regulations for the Standard of Gold and Silver Ware in the different Countries of the World. Translated from the German of STÜDNITZ by Mrs. BREWER, and Edited, with additions, by EDWIN W. STREETER.

Crown 8vo, cloth gilt and gilt edges, 7s. 6d.
The Golden Treasury of Thought:
AN ENCYCLOPÆDIA OF QUOTATIONS from Writers of all Times and Countries. Selected and Edited by THEODORE TAYLOR.

Small 8vo, cloth gilt, 6s.
Gosse's King Erik:
A Tragedy. By EDMUND W. GOSSE. With a Vignette by W. B. SCOTT.

"*The author's book, 'On Viol and Flute,' displayed such a remarkable ear for music, such a singular poetic interpretation of flowers and trees, and such-like children of Flora, and, above all, such a distinct and individual poetic savour, that it would have been a pity indeed had these good gifts been wasted in any wrong direction. In this case there is happily no cause for such pity. We have seldom seen so marked an advance in a second book beyond a first. . . . The faults of 'King Erik' are but slight matters; its merits are solid, and of a very high order.*"—ACADEMY.

Small 8vo, cloth gilt, 5s.
Gosse's On Viol and Flute.
Second Edition. With a Vignette by W. B. SCOTT.

Square 16mo, (Tauchnitz size), cloth extra, 2s. per volume.

The Golden Library:

Bayard Taylor's Diversions of the Echo Club.

The Book of Clerical Anecdotes.

Byron's Don Juan.

Carlyle (Thomas) on the Choice of Books. With a Memoir. 1s. 6d.

Emerson's Letters and Social Aims.

Godwin's (William) Lives of the Necromancers.

Holmes's Autocrat of the Breakfast Table. With an Introduction by G. A. SALA.

Holmes's Professor at the Breakfast Table.

Hood's Whims and Oddities. Complete. With all the original Illustrations.

Irving's (Washington) Tales of a Traveller.

Irving's (Washington) Tales of the Alhambra.

Jesse's (Edward) Scenes and Occupations of Country Life.

Lamb's Essays of Elia. Both Series Complete in One Volume.

Leigh Hunt's Essays: A Tale for a Chimney Corner, and other Pieces. With Portrait, and Introduction by EDMUND OLLIER.

Mallory's (Sir Thomas) Mort d'Arthur: The Stories of King Arthur and of the Knights of the Round Table. Edited by B. MONTGOMERIE RANKING.

Pascal's Provincial Letters. A New Translation, with Historical Introduction and Notes, by T. M'CRIE, D.D., LL.D.

Pope's Complete Poetical Works.

Rochefoucauld's Maxims and Moral Reflections. With Notes, and an Introductory Essay by SAINTE-BEUVE.

St. Pierre's Paul and Virginia, and the Indian Cottage. Edited, with Life, by the Rev. E. CLARKE.

Shelley's Early Poems and Queen Mab, with Essay by LEIGH HUNT.

Shelley's Later Poems: Laon and Cythna, &c.

Shelley's Posthumous Poems, the Shelley Papers, &c.

Shelley's Prose Works, including A Refutation of Deism, Zastrozzi, St. Irvyne, &c.

White's Natural History of Selborne. Edited, with additions, by THOMAS BROWN, F.L.S.

"*A series of excellently printed and carefully annotated volumes, handy in size and altogether attractive.*"—BOOKSELLER.

Crown 8vo, cloth extra, gilt, with Illustrations, 7s. 6d.
Greenwood's Low-Life Deeps.
An Account of the Strange Fish to be found there; including "The Man and Dog Fight," with much additional and confirmatory evidence; "With a Tally-Man," "A Fallen Star," "The Betting Barber," "A Coal Marriage," &c. By JAMES GREENWOOD. With Illustrations in tint by ALFRED CONCANEN.

"The book is interesting reading. It shows that there are many things in London life not dreamt of by most people. It is well got up, and contains a number of striking illustrations."—SCOTSMAN.

Crown 8vo, cloth extra, gilt, with Illustrations, 7s. 6d.
Greenwood's Wilds of London:
Descriptive Sketches, from Personal Observations and Experience, of Remarkable Scenes, People, and Places in London. By JAMES GREENWOOD. With 12 Tinted Illustrations by ALFRED CONCANEN.

"Mr. James Greenwood presents himself once more in the character of 'one whose delight it is to do his humble endeavour towards exposing and extirpating social abuses and those hole-and-corner evils which afflict society."—SATURDAY REVIEW.

Crown 8vo, cloth extra, gilt, with Illustrations, 4s. 6d.
Guyot's Earth and Man;
Or, Physical Geography in its Relation to the History of Mankind. With Additions by Professors AGASSIZ, PIERCE, and GRAY. 12 Maps and Engravings on Steel, some Coloured, and a copious Index.

Crown 8vo, cloth extra, 6s.
Hake's New Symbols:
Poems. By THOMAS GORDON HAKE.

"The entire book breathes a pure and ennobling influence, shows welcome originality of idea and illustration, and yields the highest proof of imaginative faculty and mature power of expression."—ATHENÆUM.

Medium 8vo, cloth extra, gilt, with Illustrations, 7s. 6d.
Hall's (Mrs. S. C.) Sketches of Irish
Character. With numerous Illustrations on Steel and Wood by DANIEL MACLISE, Sir JOHN GILBERT, W. HARVEY, and G. CRUIKSHANK.

"The Irish sketches of this lady resemble Miss Mitford's beautiful English Sketches in 'Our Village,' but they are far more vigorous and picturesque and bright."—BLACKWOOD'S MAGAZINE.

Demy 8vo, cloth extra, with Portrait and Illustrations, 12s.
Hawker's Memorials:
Memorials of the late Rev. ROBERT STEPHEN HAWKER, sometime Vicar of Morwenstow, in the Diocese of Exeter. Collected, arranged, and edited by the Rev. FREDERICK GEORGE LEE, D.C.L., Vicar of All Saints', Lambeth. With Photographic Portrait, Pedigree, and Illustrations.

"*Dr. Lee's 'Memorials' is a far better record of Mr. Hawker, and gives a more reverent and more true idea of the man. . . . Dr. Lee rightly confines himself to his proper subject.*"—ATHENÆUM.

Two Vols. 8vo, cloth extra, with Illustrations, 36s.
Haydon's Correspondence & Table-Talk.
With a Memoir by his Son, FREDERIC WORDSWORTH HAYDON. Comprising a large number of hitherto Unpublished Letters from KEATS, WILKIE, SOUTHEY, WORDSWORTH, KIRKUP, LEIGH HUNT, LANDSEER, HORACE SMITH, Sir G. BEAUMONT, GOETHE, Mrs. SIDDONS, Sir WALTER SCOTT, TALFOURD, JEFFREY, Miss MITFORD, MACREADY, Mrs. BROWNING, LOCKHART, HALLAM, and others. With 23 Illustrations, including Facsimiles of many nteresting Sketches, Portraits of HAYDON by KEATS and WILKIE, and HAYDON'S Portraits of WILKIE, KEATS, and MARIA FOOTE.

"*There can, we think, be no question of its interest in a purely biographical sense, or of its literary merit. The letters and table-talk form a most valuable contribution to the social and artistic history of the time.*"—PALL MALL GAZETTE.

"*The volumes are among the most interesting produced or likely to be produced by the present season.*"—EXAMINER.

"*Here we have a full-length portrait of a most remarkable man. . . . His son has done the work well—is clear and discriminating on the whole, and writes with ease and vigour. Over and above the interest that must be felt in Haydon himself, the letters afford us the opportunity of studying closely many of the greatest men and women of the time. . . . We do not hesitate to say that these letters and table-talk form a most valuable contribution to the history of art and literature in the past generation. The editor has selected and arranged them with uncommon judgment, adding many notes that contain ana and anecdotes. Every page has thus its point of interest. The book will no doubt have a wide audience, as it well deserves.*"—NONCONFORMIST.

Three Vols. royal 4to, cloth boards, £6 6s.; half-morocco, full gilt back and edges, £7 7s.
Historical Portraits ;
Upwards of 430 Engravings of Rare Prints. Comprising Collections of RODD, RICHARDSON, CAULFIELD, &c. W Descriptive Text to every Plate, giving a brief outline of the m important Historical and Biographical Facts and Dates connect with each Portrait, and references to original Authorities.

Crown 8vo, cloth extra, gilt, 7s. 6d.
Hood's (Thomas) Choice Works,
In Prose and Verse. Including the CREAM OF THE COMIC ANNUALS. With Life of the Author, Portrait, and over Two Hundred original Illustrations.

"*Not only does the volume include the better-known poems by the author, but also what is happily described as ' the Cream of the Comic Annuals.' Such delicious things as ' Don't you smell Fire ! ' ' The Parish Revolution,' and ' Huggins and Duggins,' will never want readers.*"—GRAPHIC.

"*A fair representative selection of Hood's works, many of which have been hitherto inaccessible except at high prices. Most of the best known of his comic effusions—those punning ballads in which he has never been approached—are to be found in the liberal collection Messrs. Chatto & Windus have given to the public.*"—BIRMINGHAM DAILY MAIL.

Square crown 8vo, in a handsome and specially-designed binding, gilt edges, 6s.
Hood's (Tom) From Nowhere to the
North Pole: A Noah's Arkæological Narrative. With 25 Illustrations by W. BRUNTON and E. C. BARNES.

"*Poor Tom Hood! It is very sad to turn over the droll pages of ' From Nowhere to the North Pole,' and to think that he will never make the young people, for whom, like his famous father, he ever had such a kind, sympathetic heart, laugh or cry any more. This is a birthday story, and no part of it is better than the first chapter, concerning birthdays in general, and Frank's birthday in particular. The amusing letterpress is profusely interspersed with the jingling rhymes which children love and learn so easily. Messrs. Brunton and Barnes do full justice to the writer's meaning, and a pleasanter result of the harmonious co-operation of author and artist could not be desired.*"—TIMES.

Crown 8vo, cloth extra, gilt, 7s. 6d.
Hook's (Theodore) Choice Humorous
Works, including his Ludicrous Adventures, Bons-mots, Puns, and Hoaxes. With a new Life of the Author, Portraits, Fac-similes, and Illustrations.

"*His name will be preserved. His political songs and jeux d'esprit, when the hour comes for collecting them, will form a volume of sterling and lasting attraction; and after many clever romances of this age shall have sufficiently occupied public attention, and sunk, like hundreds of former generations, into utter oblivion, there are tales in his collection which will be read with even a greater interest than they commanded in their novelty.*"—J. G. LOCKHART.

Two Vols. royal 8vo, with Coloured Frontispieces, cloth extra, £2 5s.
Hope's Costume of the Ancients.
Illustrated in upwards of 320 Outline Engravings, containing Representations of Egyptian, Greek, and Roman Habits and Dresses.

"*The substance of many expensive works, containing all that may be necessary to give to artists, and even to dramatic performers and to others engaged in classical representations, an idea of ancient costumes sufficiently ample to prevent their offending in their performances by gross and obvious blunders.*"

Crown 8vo, cloth extra, 7s.

Horne's Orion:
An Epic Poem, in Three Books. By RICHARD HENGIST HORNE. With Photographic Portrait. Tenth Edition.

"*Orion will be admitted, by every man of genius, to be one of the noblest, if not the very noblest poetical work of the age. Its defects are trivial and conventional, its beauties intrinsic and supreme.*"—EDGAR ALLAN POE.

Atlas folio, half morocco gilt, £5 5s.

The Italian Masters:
Autotype Facsimiles of Original Drawings in the British Museum. With Critical and Descriptive Notes, Biographical and Artistic, by J. COMYNS CARR.

Crown 8vo, cloth extra, with Illustrations, 10s. 6d.

Jennings' The Rosicrucians:
Their Rites and Mysteries. With Chapters on the Ancient Fire and Serpent Worshippers, and Explanations of Mystic Symbols in Monuments and Talismans of Primæval Philosophers. By HARGRAVE JENNINGS. With upwards of 300 Illustrations.

Small 8vo, cloth extra, 6s.

Jeux d'Esprit,
Written and Spoken, of the Later Wits and Humourists. Collected and Edited by HENRY S. LEIGH.

Two Vols. 8vo, with 52 Illustrations and Maps, cloth extra, gilt, 14s.

Josephus's Complete Works.
Translated by WHISTON. Containing both "The Antiquities of the Jews" and "The Wars of the Jews."

"*This admirable translation far exceeds all preceding ones, and has never be equalled by any subsequent attempt of the kind.*"—LOWNDES.

Small 8vo, cloth, full gilt, gilt edges, with Illustrations, 6s.

Kavanaghs' Pearl Fountain,
And other Fairy Stories. By BRIDGET and JULIA KAVANAGH. With Thirty Illustrations by J. MOYR SMITH.

Two Vols. crown 8vo, cloth extra, 21s.

Kingsley's Fireside Studies:
Essays. By HENRY KINGSLEY.

"*These 'Fireside Studies' show Mr. Kingsley at his very best. Their pervading charms are their freshness and liveliness. The volumes are delightful.*"—TIMES.

Crown 8vo, cloth extra, gilt, with Portraits, 7s. 6d.

Lamb's Complete Works,

In Prose and Verse, reprinted from the Original Editions, with many Pieces hitherto unpublished. Edited, with Notes and Introduction, by R. H. SHEPHERD. With Two Portraits and Facsimile of a page of the "Essay on Roast Pig."

"*The genius of Mr. Lamb, as developed in his various writings, takes rank with the most original of the age. As a critic he stands facile princeps in the subjects he handled. Search English literature through, from its first beginnings until now, and you will find none like him. There is not a criticism he ever wrote that does not directly tell you a number of things you had no previous notion of. In criticism he was, indeed, in all senses of the word, a discoverer—like Vasco, Nunez, or Magellan. In that very domain of literature with which you fancied yourself most variously and closely acquainted, he would show you 'fresh fields and pastures new,' and these the most fruitful and delightful. For the riches he discovered were richer that they had lain so deep—the more valuable were they, when found, that they had eluded the search of ordinary men. As an essayist, Charles Lamb will be remembered in years to come with Rabelais and Montaigne, with Sir Thomas Browne, with Steele and with Addison. He unites many of the finest characteristics of these several writers. He has wisdom and wit of the highest order, exquisite humour, a genuine and cordial vein of pleasantry, and the most heart-touching pathos. In the largest acceptation of the word, he is a humanist.*"—JOHN FORSTER.

Crown 8vo, cloth extra, with numerous Illustrations, 10s. 6d.

Mary & Charles Lamb:

Their Poems, Letters and Remains. With Reminiscences and Notes by W. CAREW HAZLITT. With HANCOCK'S Portrait of the Essayist, Facsimiles of the Title-pages of the rare First Editions of Lamb's and Coleridge's Works, and numerous Illustrations.

"*Must be consulted by all future biographers of the Lambs.*"—DAILY NEWS.
"*Very many passages will delight those fond of literary trifles; hardly any portion will fail in interest for lovers of Charles Lamb and his sister.*"—STANDARD.

Post 8vo, cloth extra, with Portrait and Map, 9s.

Lee's (General) Life and Campaigns.

By his Nephew, EDWARD LEE CHILDE. With Steel-plate Portrait by JEENS, and a Map.

"*A valuable and well-written contribution to the history of the Civil War in the United States.*"—SATURDAY REVIEW.
"*As a clear and compendious survey of a life of the true heroic type, Mr. Childe's volume may well be commended to the English reader.*"—GRAPHIC.

Crown 8vo, cloth extra, with Illustrations, 7s. 6d.

Life in London;

Or, The History of Jerry Hawthorn and Corinthian Tom. With the whole of CRUIKSHANK'S Illustrations, in Colours, after the Originals.

Demy 8vo, cloth extra, with Maps and Illustrations, 18s.
Lamont's Yachting in the Arctic Seas;
or, Notes of Five Voyages of Sport and Discovery in the Neighbourhood of Spitzbergen and Novaya Zemlya. By JAMES LAMONT, F.R.G.S. With numerous full-page Illustrations by Dr. LIVESAY.

"*After wading through numberless volumes of icy fiction, concocted narrative, and spurious biography of Arctic voyagers, it is pleasant to meet with a real and genuine volume. . . . He shows much tact in recounting his adventures, and they are so interspersed with anecdotes and information as to make them anything but wearisome. . . . The book, as a whole, is the most important addition made to our Arctic literature for a long time.*"—ATHENÆUM.

"*Full of entertainment and information.*"—NATURE.

Small crown 8vo, cloth extra, 4s. 6d.
Linton's Joshua Davidson,
Christian and Communist. By E. LYNN LINTON. Sixth Edition, with a New Preface.

"*In a short and vigorous preface, Mrs. Linton defends her notion of the logical outcome of Christianity as embodied in this attempt to conceive how Christ would have acted, with whom He would have fraternised, and who would have declined to receive Him, had He appeared in the present generation.*"—EXAMINER.

Crown 8vo, cloth extra, with Illustrations, 7s. 6d.
Longfellow's Complete Prose Works.
Including "Outre Mer," "Hyperion," "Kavanagh," "The Poets and Poetry of Europe," and "Driftwood." With Portrait and Illustrations by VALENTINE BROMLEY.

*** *This is by far the most complete edition ever issued in this country. "Outre-Mer" contains two additional chapters, restored from the first edition; while "The Poets and Poetry of Europe," and the little collection of Sketches entitled "Driftwood," are now first introduced to the English Public.*

Crown 8vo, cloth extra, gilt, with Illustrations, 7s. 6d.
Longfellow's Poetical Works.
Carefully Reprinted from the Original Editions. With numerous fine Illustrations on Steel and Wood.

"*Mr. Longfellow has for many years been the best known and the most read of American poets; and his popularity is of the right kind, and rightly and fairly won. He has not stooped to catch attention by artifice, nor striven to force it by violence. His works have faced the test of parody and burlesque (which in these days is almost the common lot of writings of any mark), and have come off unharmed.*"—SATURDAY REVIEW.

Crown 8vo, cloth extra, 6s. 6d.
Lost Beauties of the English Language:
An Appeal to Authors, Poets, Clergymen, and Public Speakers. By CHARLES MACKAY, LL.D.

THE FRASER PORTRAITS.—Demy 4to, cloth gilt and gilt edges, with
83 characteristic Portraits, 31s. 6d.
Maclise's Gallery of Illustrious Literary
Characters. With Notes by Dr. MAGINN. Edited, with copious
Additional Notes, by WILLIAM BATES, B.A.
"*One of the most interesting volumes of this year's literature.*"—TIMES.
"*Deserves a place on every drawing-room table, and may not unfitly be removed from the drawing-room to the library.*"—SPECTATOR.

Crown 8vo, cloth extra, with Illustrations, 2s. 6d.
Madre Natura v. The Moloch of Fashion.
By LUKE LIMNER. With 32 Illustrations by the Author.
FOURTH EDITION, revised and enlarged.
"*Agreeably written and amusingly illustrated. Common sense and erudition are brought to bear on the subjects discussed in it.*"—LANCET.

Handsomely printed in facsimile, price 5s.
Magna Charta.
An exact Facsimile of the Original Document in the British Museum, printed on fine plate paper, nearly 3 feet long by 2 feet wide, with the Arms and Seals of the Barons emblazoned in Gold and Colours.

** A full Translation, with Notes, on a large sheet, 6d.

Small 8vo, cloth extra, 7s. 6d.
Mark Twain's The Adventures of Tom Sawyer.
"*The earlier part of the book is to our thinking the most amusing thing Mark Twain has written. The humour is not always uproarious, but it is always genuine, and sometimes almost pathetic.*"—ATHENÆUM.
"*A book to be read. There is a certain freshness and novelty about it, a practically romantic character, so to speak, which will make it very attractive.*"—SPECTATOR.
"*From a novel so replete with good things, and one so full of significance, as it brings before us what we can feel is the real spirit of home life in the Far West, there is no possibility of obtaining extracts which will convey to the reader any idea of the purport of the book. . . . The book will no doubt be a great favourite with boys, for whom it must in good part have been intended; but next to boys, we should say that it might be most prized by philosophers and poets.*"—EXAMINER.
"*Will delight all the lads who may get hold of it. We have made the experiment upon a youngster, and found that the reading of the book brought on constant peals of laughter.*"—SCOTSMAN.

Crown 8vo, cloth extra, with Illustrations, 7s. 6d.
Mark Twain's Choice Works.
Revised and Corrected throughout by the Author. With Life, Portrait, and numerous Illustrations.

Post 8vo, illustrated boards, 2s.
Mark Twain's Pleasure Trip on the
Continent of Europe. ("The Innocents Abroad," and "The New Pilgrim's Progress.")

Two Vols. crown 8vo, cloth extra, 18s.

Marston's (Dr. Westland) Dramatic
and Poetical Works. Collected Library Edition.

"*The 'Patrician's Daughter' is an oasis in the desert of modern dramatic literature, a real emanation of mind. We do not recollect any modern work in which states of thought are so freely developed, except the 'Torquato Tasso' of Goethe. The play is a work of art in the same sense that a play of Sophocles is a work of art; it is one simple idea in a state of gradual development . . . 'The Favourite of Fortune' is one of the most important additions to the stock of English prose comedy that has been made during the present century.*"—TIMES.

Crown 8vo, cloth extra, 8s.

Marston's (Philip B.) All in All:
Poems and Sonnets.

"*Many of these poems are leavened with the leaven of genuine poetical sentiment, and expressed with grace and beauty of language. A tender melancholy, as well as a penetrating pathos, gives character to much of their sentiment, and lends it an irresistible interest to all who can feel.*"—STANDARD.

Crown 8vo, cloth extra, 8s.

Marston's (Philip B.) Song Tide,
And other Poems. Second Edition.

"*This is a first work of extraordinary performance and of still more extraordinary promise. The youngest school of English poetry has received an important accession to its ranks in Philip Bourke Marston.*"—EXAMINER.

Crown 8vo, cloth extra, gilt, gilt edges, 7s. 6d.

Muses of Mayfair;
Vers de Société of the Nineteenth Century. Including Selections from TENNYSON, BROWNING, SWINBURNE, ROSSETTI, JEAN INGELOW, LOCKER, INGOLDSBY, HOOD, LYTTON, C. S. C.; LANDOR, AUSTIN DOBSON, HENRY S. LEIGH, &c., &c. Edited by H. CHOLMONDELEY-PENNELL.

Crown 8vo, cloth extra, with Vignette Portraits, price 6s. per Vol.

The Old Dramatists:

Ben Jonson's Works.
With Notes, Critical and Explanatory, and a Biographical Memoir by WILLIAM GIFFORD. Edited by Col. CUNNINGHAM. Three Vols.

Chapman's Works.
Now First Collected. Complete in Three Vols. Vol. I. contains the Plays complete, including the doubtful ones; Vol. II. the Poems and Minor Translations, with an Introductory Essay by ALGERNON CHARLES SWINBURNE; Vol. III. the Translations of the Iliad and Odyssey.

Marlowe's Works.
Including his Translations. Edited, with Notes and Introduction, by Col. CUNNINGHAM. One Vol.

Massinger's Plays.
From the Text of WILLIAM GIFFORD. With the addition of the Tragedy of "Believe as you List." Edited by Col. CUNNINGHAM. One Vol.

Fcap. 8vo, cloth extra, 6s.
O'Shaughnessy's (Arthur) An Epic of
Women, and other Poems. Second Edition.

Crown 8vo, cloth extra, 10s. 6d.
O'Shaughnessy's Lays of France.
(Founded on the "Lays of Marie.") Second Edition.

Fcap. 8vo, cloth extra, 7s. 6d.
O'Shaughnessy's Music and Moonlight:
Poems and Songs.

"*It is difficult to say which is more exquisite, the technical perfection of structure and melody, or the delicate pathos of thought. Mr. O'Shaughnessy will enrich our literature with some of the very best songs written in our generation.*"—ACADEMY.

Crown 8vo, carefully printed on creamy paper, and tastefully bound in cloth for the Library, price 6s. each.
The Piccadilly Novels:
POPULAR STORIES BY THE BEST AUTHORS.

Antonina. By WILKIE COLLINS.
Illustrated by Sir J. GILBERT and ALFRED CONCANEN.

Basil. By WILKIE COLLINS.
Illustrated by Sir JOHN GILBERT and J. MAHONEY.

Hide and Seek. By WILKIE COLLINS.
Illustrated by Sir JOHN GILBERT and J. MAHONEY.

The Dead Secret. By WILKIE COLLINS.
Illustrated by Sir JOHN GILBERT and H. FURNISS.

Queen of Hearts. By WILKIE COLLINS.
Illustrated by Sir J. GILBERT and A. CONCANEN.

My Miscellanies. By WILKIE COLLINS.
With Steel Portrait, and Illustrations by A. CONCANEN.

The Woman in White. By WILKIE COLLINS.
Illustrated by Sir J. GILBERT and F. A. FRASER.

The Moonstone. By WILKIE COLLINS.
Illustrated by G. DU MAURIER and F. A. FRASER.

Man and Wife. By WILKIE COLLINS.
Illustrated by WILLIAM SMALL.

THE PICCADILLY NOVELS—*continued.*

Poor Miss Finch. By WILKIE COLLINS.
Illustrated by G. DU MAURIER and EDWARD HUGHES.

Miss or Mrs.? By WILKIE COLLINS.
Illustrated by S. L. FILDES and HENRY WOODS.

The New Magdalen. By WILKIE COLLINS.
Illustrated by G. DU MAURIER and C. S. RANDS.

The Frozen Deep. By WILKIE COLLINS.
Illustrated by G. DU MAURIER and J. MAHONEY.

The Law and the Lady. By WILKIE COLLINS.
Illustrated by S. L. FILDES and S. HALL.

"*Like all the author's works, full of a certain power and ingenuity. . . . It is upon such suggestions of crime that the fascination of the story depends. . . . The reader feels it his duty to serve to the end upon the inquest on which he has been called by the author.*"—TIMES.

Felicia. By M. BETHAM EDWARDS.

"*A noble novel. Its teaching is elevated, its story is sympathetic, and the kind of feeling its perusal leaves behind is that more ordinarily derived from music or poetry than from prose fiction. Few works in modern fiction stand as high in our estimation as this.*"—SUNDAY TIMES.

Patricia Kemball. By E. LYNN LINTON.
With Frontispiece by G. DU MAURIER.

"*A very clever and well-constructed story, original and striking, interesting all through. A novel abounding in thought and power and interest.*"—TIMES.

"*Displays genuine humour, as well as keen social observation. Enough graphic portraiture and witty observation to furnish materials for half-a-dozen novels of the ordinary kind.*"—SATURDAY REVIEW.

The Atonement of Leam Dundas. By E. LYNN LINTON.

"*In her narrowness and her depth, in her boundless loyalty, her self-forgetting passion, that exclusiveness of love which is akin to cruelty, and the fierce humility which is vicarious pride, Leam Dundas is a striking figure. In one quality the authoress has in some measure surpassed herself.*"—PALL MALL GAZETTE.

The Evil Eye, and other Stories. By KATHARINE S. MACQUOID.
Illustrated by THOMAS R. MACQUOID and PERCY MACQUOID.

"*For Norman country life what the 'Johnny Ludlow' stories are for English rural delineation, that is, cameos delicately, if not very minutely or vividly wrought, and quite finished enough to give a pleasurable sense of artistic ease and faculty. A word of commendation is merited by the illustrations.*"—ACADEMY.

Number Seventeen. By HENRY KINGSLEY.

Oakshott Castle. By HENRY KINGSLEY.

"*A brisk and clear north wind of sentiment—sentiment that braces instead of enervating—blows through all his works, and makes all their readers at once healthier and more glad.*"—SPECTATOR.

THE PICCADILLY NOVELS—*continued*.

Open! Sesame! By FLORENCE MARRYAT.
Illustrated by F. A. FRASER.
"A story which arouses and sustains the reader's interest to a higher degree than, perhaps, any of its author's former works. . . . A very excellent story."—GRAPHIC.

Whiteladies. By Mrs. OLIPHANT.
With Illustrations by A. HOPKINS and H. WOODS.
"Is really a pleasant and readable book, written with practical ease and grace."—TIMES.

The Best of Husbands. By JAMES PAYN.
Illustrated by J. MOYR SMITH.

Walter's Word. By JAMES PAYN.
Illustrated by J. MOYR SMITH.

Halves, and other Stories. By JAMES PAYN.
"His novels are always commendable in the sense of art. They also possess another distinct claim to our liking: the girls in them are remarkably charming and true to nature, as most people, we believe, have the good fortune to observe nature represented by girls."—SPECTATOR.

The Way we Live Now. By ANTHONY TROLLOPE.
With Illustrations.
"Mr. Trollope has a true artist's idea of tone, of colour, of harmony: his pictures are one, and seldom out of drawing; he never strains after effect, is fidelity itself in expressing English life, is never guilty of caricature."— FORTNIGHTLY REVIEW.

Diamond Cut Diamond. By T. A. TROLLOPE.
"The indefinable charm of Tuscan and Venetian life breathes in his pages." —TIMES.
"Full of life, of interest, of close observation, and sympathy. . . . When Mr. Trollope paints a scene it is sure to be a scene worth painting."—SATURDAY REVIEW.

Bound to the Wheel. By JOHN SAUNDERS.

Guy Waterman. By JOHN SAUNDERS.

One Against the World. By JOHN SAUNDERS.

The Lion in the Path. By JOHN SAUNDERS.
"A carefully written and beautiful story—a story of goodness and truth, which is yet as interesting as though it dealt with the opposite qualities. . . . The author of this really clever story has been at great pains to work out all its details with elaborate conscientiousness, and the result is a very vivid picture of the ways of life and habits of thought of a hundred and fifty years ago. . . Certainly a very interesting book."—TIMES.

Crown 8vo, red cloth, extra, 5s. each.

Ouida's Novels.—Uniform Edition.

Folle Farine. By Ouida.
Idalia. By Ouida.
Chandos. By Ouida.
Under Two Flags. By Ouida.
Tricotrin. By Ouida.
Cecil Castlemaine's Gage. By Ouida.
Held in Bondage. By Ouida.
Pascarel. By Ouida.
Puck. By Ouida.
Dog of Flanders. By Ouida.
Strathmore. By Ouida.
Two Little Wooden Shoes. By Ouida.
Signa. By Ouida.
In a Winter City. By Ouida.

"Keen poetic insight, an intense love of nature, a deep admiration of the beautiful in form and colour, are the gifts of Ouida."—Morning Post.

Mr. Wilkie Collins's New Novel.—Two Vols. crown 8vo, 21s.

The Two Destinies:

A Romance. By Wilkie Collins, Author of "The Woman in White."

"*Curious, clever, here and there of absorbing interest.*"—Nonconformist.
"*As full of absorbing interest as 'The Woman in White.' With practised art and all his old lucidity of style, Mr. Collins excites the reader's interest in the very first chapter. A strong vein of the supernatural runs through 'The Two Destinies,' which cannot fail to be read with intense interest.*"—Illustrated News.
"*Admirers of the author's remarkable constructive skill, among which multitude we may claim a forward place, will begin his new work with keener interest than usual when they see from the dedication that it has satisfied so exacting a critic as Mr. Charles Reade, who, we are informed, has been pleased to be interested by a 'certain novelty of design and treatment' found in it.*"—Manchester Examiner.

New Novel by Dr. Sandwith.—Three Vols. cr. 8vo, 31s. 6d.

Minsterborough:

A Tale of English Life. By Humphry Sandwith, C.B., D.C.L.

"*It is a long time since we have read anything so refreshing as the novel to the composition of which Mr. Sandwith has been devoting such time and labour as could be spared from the more serious duties of an apostle of Democracy and clean water. Everything in the book is so delightfully straightforward. We are never bothered with subtle analysis of character, or with dark suggestions that things are other than they seem. . . . The story is not at all badly told.*"—Athenæum.

Jean Middlemass's New Novel.—Three Vols. crown 8vo, 31s. 6d.

Mr. Dorillion:

A Novel. By Jean Middlemass, Author of "Wild Georgie."

"*This is quite the best novel which Miss Middlemass has written. The story is well conceived, well told, full of strong situations, and rich in surprises; the characters speak, act, and think like human beings, and the style is uniformly lively and well sustained.*"—World.

A NEW WRITER.—Three Vols. crown 8vo, 31s. 6d.

The Democracy:
A Novel. By WHYTE THORNE.

"*A very careful, and in many respects very praiseworthy story.*"—SATURDAY REVIEW.

"*It is always difficult for anyone not personally concerned in English politics to write about them without making serious blunders; but the author of the novel before us keeps clear of error, and writes pleasantly enough.*"—ATHENÆUM.

MRS. MACQUOID'S NEW NOVEL.—Three Vols. crown 8vo, 31s. 6d.

Lost Rose;
and other Stories. By KATHARINE S. MACQUOID.

T. A. TROLLOPE'S NEW NOVEL.—Three Vols. crown 8vo, 31s. 6d.

A Family Party in the Piazza of St. Peter's. By T. ADOLPHUS TROLLOPE. [*In the press.*

NEW NOVEL BY JAMES GREENWOOD.—3 vols. crown 8vo, 31s. 6d.

Dick Temple.
By JAMES GREENWOOD. [*In the press.*

Two Vols. 8vo, cloth extra, with Illustrations, 10s. 6d.

Plutarch's Lives of Illustrious Men.
Translated from the Greek, with Notes Critical and Historical, and a Life of Plutarch, by JOHN and WILLIAM LANGHORNE. New Edition, with Medallion Portraits.

"*When I write, I care not to have books about me; but I can hardly be without a 'Plutarch.'*"—MONTAIGNE.

Crown 8vo, cloth extra, with Portrait and Illustrations, 7s. 6d.

Poe's Choice Prose and Poetical Works.
With BAUDELAIRE'S "Essay."

"*Poe's great power lay in writing tales, which rank in a class by themselves, and have their characteristics strongly defined.*"—FRASER'S MAGAZINE.

"*Poe stands as much alone among verse-writers as Salvator Rosa among painters.*"—SPECTATOR.

Small 8vo, cloth extra, with Illustrations, 3s. 6d.

The Prince of Argolis:
A Story of the Old Greek Fairy Time. By J. MOYR SMITH. With 130 Illustrations by the Author.

Crown 8vo, cloth extra, with Portrait and Facsimile, 12s. 6d.

The Final Reliques of Father Prout.

Collected and Edited, from MSS. supplied by the family of the Rev. FRANCIS MAHONY, by BLANCHARD JERROLD.

"*We heartily commend this handsome volume to all lovers of sound wit, genuine humour, and manly sense.*"—SPECTATOR.

"*Sparkles all over, and is full of interest. Mahony, like Sydney Smith, could write on no subject without being brilliant and witty.*"—BRITISH QUARTERLY REVIEW.

"*It is well that the present long-delayed volume should remind a younger generation of his fame. . . . The charming letters from Paris, Florence, and Rome . . . are the most perfect specimens of what a foreign correspondence ought to be.*"—ACADEMY.

In Two Series, small 4to, blue and gold, gilt edges, 6s. each.

Puniana ;

or, Thoughts Wise and Other-Why's. A New Collection of Riddles, Conundrums, Jokes, Sells, &c. In Two Series, each containing 3000 of the best Riddles, 10,000 most outrageous Puns, and upwards of Fifty beautifully executed Drawings by the Editor, the Hon. HUGH ROWLEY. Each Series is complete in itself.

"*A witty, droll, and most amusing work, profusely and elegantly illustrated.*" —STANDARD.

Crown 8vo, cloth extra, gilt, 7s. 6d.

The Pursuivant of Arms ;

or, Heraldry founded upon Facts. A Popular Guide to the Science of Heraldry. By J. R. PLANCHÉ, Esq., Somerset Herald. To which are added, Essays on the BADGES OF THE HOUSES OF LANCASTER AND YORK. With Coloured Frontispiece, five full-page Plates, and about 200 Illustrations.

Crown 8vo, cloth extra, 7s. 6d.

Rabelais' Works.

Faithfully Translated from the French, with variorum Notes, and numerous Characteristic Illustrations by GUSTAVE DORÉ.

Handsomely printed, price 5s.

The Roll of Battle Abbey ;

Or, a List of the Principal Warriors who came over from Normandy with William the Conqueror, and Settled in this Country, A.D. 1066-7. Printed on fine plate paper, nearly three feet by two, with the principal Arms emblazoned in Gold and Colours.

In 4to, very handsomely printed, extra gold cloth, 12s.

The Roll of Caerlaverock,

The Oldest Heraldic Roll; including the Original Anglo-Norman Poem, and an English Translation of the MS. in the British Museum. By THOMAS WRIGHT, M.A. The Arms emblazoned in Gold and Colours.

NEW AND POPULAR EDITION OF "SANSON'S MEMOIRS."—One Vol. crown 8vo, cloth extra, 7s. 6d.

Memoirs of the Sanson Family:

Seven Generations of Executioners. Compiled from Private Documents in the possession of the Family. By HENRI SANSON. Translated from the French, with an Introduction, by CAMILLE BARRÈRE.

"*A faithful translation of this curious work, which will certainly repay perusal —not on the ground of its being full of horrors, for the original author seems to be rather ashamed of the technical aspect of his profession, and is commendably reticent as to its details, but because it contains a lucid account of the most notable causes célèbres from the time of Louis XIV. to a period within the memory of persons still living. . . . Can scarcely fail to be extremely entertaining.*"— DAILY TELEGRAPH.

Crown 8vo, cloth extra, profusely Illustrated, 4s. 6d. each.

The "Secret Out" Series.

The Volumes are as follows:

The Art of Amusing:
A Collection of Graceful Arts, Games, Tricks, Puzzles, and Charades. By FRANK BELLEW. 300 Illustrations.

Hanky-Panky:
Very Easy Tricks, Very Difficult Tricks, White Magic, Sleight of Hand. Edited by W. H. CREMER. 200 Illustrations.

Magician's Own Book:
Performances with Cups and Balls, Eggs, Hats, Handkerchiefs, &c. All from Actual Experience. Edited by W. H. CREMER. 200 Illustrations.

Magic No Mystery.
Tricks with Cards, Dice, Balls, &c., with fully descriptive Directions; the Art of Secret Writing; the Training of Performing Animals, &c. With Coloured Frontispiece and many Illustrations.

The Merry Circle:
A Book of New Intellectual Games and Amusements. By CLARA BELLEW. Many Illustrations.

The Secret Out:
One Thousand Tricks with Cards, and other Recreations; with Entertaining Experiments in Drawing-room or "White Magic." By W. H. CREMER. 300 Engravings.

Post 8vo, with Illustrations, cloth extra, gilt edges, 18s.

The Lansdowne Shakespeare.

Beautifully printed in red and black, in small but very clear type. With engraved facsimile of DROESHOUT's Portrait, and 37 beautiful Steel Plates, after STOTHARD.

BOOKS PUBLISHED BY

In reduced facsimile, small 8vo, half Roxburghe, 10s. 6d.
The First Folio Shakespeare.
Mr. WILLIAM SHAKESPEARE'S Comedies, Histories, and Tragedies. Published according to the true Originall Copies. London, Printed by ISAAC IAGGARD and ED. BLOUNT, 1623.—An exact Reproduction of the extremely rare original, in reduced facsimile by a photographic process—ensuring the strictest accuracy in every detail. *A full prospectus will be sent upon application.*

"*To Messrs. Chatto and Windus belongs the merit of having done more to facilitate the critical study of the text of our great dramatist than all the Shakespeare clubs and societies put together. A complete facsimile of the celebrated First Folio edition of 1623 for half-a-guinea is at once a miracle of cheapness and enterprise. Being in a reduced form, the type is necessarily rather diminutive, but it is as distinct as in a genuine copy of the original, and will be found to be as useful and far more handy to the student than the latter.*"—ATHENÆUM.

Two Vols. crown 8vo, cloth extra, 18s.
The School of Shakespeare.
Including "The Life and Death of Captain Thomas Stukeley," with a New Life of Stucley, from Unpublished Sources; "A Warning for Fair Women," with a Reprint of the Account of the Murder; "Nobody and Somebody;" "The Cobbler's Prophecy;" "Histriomastix;" "The Prodigal Son," &c. Edited, with Introductions and Notes, by RICHARD SIMPSON.

Crown 8vo, cloth extra, gilt, with 10 full-page Tinted Illustrations, 7s. 6d.
Sheridan's Complete Works,
with Life and Anecdotes. Including his Dramatic Writings, printed from the Original Editions, his Works in Prose and Poetry, Translations, Speeches, Jokes, Puns, &c.; with a Collection of Sheridaniana.

"*The editor has brought together within a manageable compass not only the seven plays by which Sheridan is best known, but a collection also of his poetical pieces which are less familiar to the public, sketches of unfinished dramas, selections from his reported witticisms, and extracts from his principal speeches. To these is prefixed a short but well-written memoir, giving the chief facts in Sheridan's literary and political career; so that, with this volume in his hand, the student may consider himself tolerably well furnished with all that is necessary for a general comprehension of the subject of it.*"—PALL MALL GAZETTE.

Crown 8vo, cloth extra, with Illustrations, 7s. 6d.
Signboards:
Their History. With Anecdotes of Famous Taverns and Remarkable Characters. By JACOB LARWOOD and JOHN CAMDEN HOTTEN. With nearly 100 Illustrations.

"*Even if we were ever so maliciously inclined, we could not pick out all Messrs. Larwood and Hotten's plums, because the good things are so numerous as to defy the most wholesale depredation.*"—TIMES.

Crown 8vo, cloth extra, gilt, 6s. 6d.

The Slang Dictionary:

Etymological, Historical, and Anecdotal. An ENTIRELY NEW EDITION, revised throughout, and considerably Enlarged.

"*We are glad to see the Slang Dictionary reprinted and enlarged. From a high scientific point of view this book is not to be despised. Of course it cannot fail to be amusing also. It contains the very vocabulary of unrestrained humour, and oddity, and grotesqueness. In a word, it provides valuable material both for the student of language and the student of human nature.*"—ACADEMY.

Exquisitely printed in miniature, cloth extra, gilt edges, 2s. 6d.

The Smoker's Text-Book.

By J. HAMER, F.R.S.L.

Crown 8vo, cloth extra, 9s.

Stedman's Victorian Poets;

Critical Essays. By EDMUND CLARENCE STEDMAN.

"*We ought to be thankful to those who do critical work with competent skill and understanding, with honesty of purpose, and with diligence and thoroughness of execution. And Mr. Stedman, having chosen to work in this line, deserves the thanks of English scholars by these qualities and by something more; .... he is faithful, studious, and discerning.*"—SATURDAY REVIEW.

Imperial 4to, containing 150 beautifully-finished full-page Engravings and Nine Vignettes, all tinted, and some illuminated in gold and colours, half-morocco, £9 9s.

Stothard's Monumental Effigies of Great

Britain. With Historical Description and Introduction, by JOHN KEMPE, F.S.A. A NEW EDITION, with a large body of Additional Notes by JOHN HEWITT.

"*A new edition of Stothard is quite an era in Archæology, and we welcome it the more because two of the most industrious members of the Archæological Institute have contributed greatly to its augmentation and improvement. The work has been reproduced by Messrs. Chatto & Windus, with many additional notes by Mr. Hewitt. In order to the production of these notes, Mr. Hewitt visited almost all the monuments drawn by Stothard, and the result of his examinations was a constant subject of discussion between himself and Mr. Albert Way, to which we owe the large amount of additamenta in the new edition now before us. To Stothard's work, more than to any other, may perhaps be attributed the great revival of taste and feeling for the monuments of our ancestors which the present generation has seen. The interest of the subject is of the most universal character, and this new edition of Stothard is sure to be very popular. It will be a great satisfaction to our readers to find that the result of recent Archæological Investigations upon such subjects have been carefully brought together in the work under consideration. Besides the exhaustive account of the effigies themselves, the work as it now stands includes a concise history of mediæval costume, of monumental architecture, sculpture, brass engraving, and the numerous topics arising from the review of a series of examples extending from the twelfth to the sixteeth century. Foreign as well as English monuments have been called into requisition to illustrate the numerous points discussed in the work.*"—ARCHÆOLOGICAL JOURNAL, June, 1876.

*** A few Large Paper copies, royal folio, with all the coats of arms illuminated in gold and colours, and the plates very carefully finished in body-colours, heightened with gold in the very finest style, half-morocco, £15 15s.

Large 8vo, half-Roxburghe, with Illustrations, price 9s.

Stow's Survey of London.

Edited by W. J. THOMS, F.S.A. A New Edition, with Copperplate Illustrations.

Crown 8vo, cloth extra, with Illustrations, 7s. 6d.

Swift's Choice Works,

in Prose and Verse. With Memoir, Portrait, and Facsimiles of the Maps in the Original Edition of "Gulliver's Travels."

"The 'Tale of a Tub' is, in my apprehension, the masterpiece of Swift; certainly Rabelais has nothing superior, even in invention, nor anything so condensed, so pointed, so full of real meaning, of biting satire, of felicitous analogy. The 'Battle of the Books' is such an improvement on the similar combat in the Lutrin, that we can hardly own it as an imitation."—HALLAM.

"Swift's reputation as a poet has been in a manner obscured by the greater splendour, by the natural force and inventive genius, of his prose writings; but, if he had never written either the 'Tale of a Tub' or 'Gulliver's Travels,' his name merely as a poet would have come down to us, and have gone down to posterity, with well-earned honours."—HAZLITT.

Mr. Swinburne's Works:

The Queen Mother and Rosamond. Fcap. 8vo, 5s.

Atalanta in Calydon.
A New Edition. Crown 8vo, 6s.

Chastelard.
A Tragedy. Fcap. 8vo, 7s.

Poems and Ballads.
Fcap. 8vo, 9s.

Notes on "Poems and Ballads." 8vo, 1s.

William Blake:
A Critical Essay. With Facsimile Paintings. Demy 8vo, 16s.

Songs before Sunrise.
Crown 8vo, 10s. 6d.

Bothwell.
A Tragedy. Two Vols. crown 8vo, 12s. 6d.

George Chapman:
An Essay. Crown 8vo, 7s.

Songs of Two Nations.
Crown 8vo, 6s.

Essays and Studies.
Crown 8vo, 12s.

Erechtheus:
A Tragedy. Crown 8vo, 6s.

"The easy sweep of his flowing verse suggests anything rather than the idea of effort. Nor have we ever seen him stronger than in this poem of 'ERECHTHEUS;' while no one can say, as they are borne along with his melodious numbers, that he has been betrayed into sacrificing meaning to sound. He seems to have caught the enthusiasm of a congenial subject; to have been carried back to the spirit of an heroic age, to have fired his fancy with the thoughts and sensations that might have animated the soul of a god-born Athenian in the supreme crisis of his country's fate. . . . Never before has Mr. Swinburne shown himself more masterly in his choruses; magnificent in their fire and spirit, they have more than the usual graces of diction and smoothness of melody. . . . The best proof of the winning beauty of these choruses is the extreme reluctance with which you bring yourself to a pause in the course of quotation. You feel it almost sacrilegious to detach the gems, and it is with a sense of your ruthless Vandalism that you shatter the artist's setting."—EDINBURGH REVIEW, July, 1876, in a review of "Erechtheus."

Fcap. 8vo, cloth extra, 3s. 6d.

Rossetti's (W. M.) Criticism upon Swinburne's "Poems and Ballads."

Crown 8vo, cloth extra, with Illustrations, 7s. 6d.

Strutt's Sports and Pastimes of the

People of England; including the Rural and Domestic Recreations, May Games, Mummeries, Shows, Processions, Pageants, and Pompous Spectacles, from the Earliest Period to the Present Time. With 140 Illustrations. Edited by WILLIAM HONE.

⁎⁎ A few Large Paper Copies, with an extra set of Copperplate Illustrations, carefully coloured by hand, from the Originals, 50s.

Medium 8vo, cloth extra, with Illustrations, 7s. 6d.

Dr. Syntax's Three Tours,

in Search of the Picturesque, in Search of Consolation, and in Search of a Wife. With the whole of ROWLANDSON'S droll full-page Illustrations, in Colours, and Life of the Author by J. C. HOTTEN.

Large post 8vo, cloth, full gilt, gilt top, with Illustrations, 12s. 6d.

Thackerayana:

Notes and Anecdotes. Illustrated by a profusion of Sketches by WILLIAM MAKEPEACE THACKERAY, depicting Humorous Incidents in his School-life, and Favourite Characters in the books of his everyday reading. With Hundreds of Wood Engravings and Five Coloured Plates, from Mr. Thackeray's Original Drawings.

"*It would have been a real loss to bibliographical literature had copyright difficulties deprived the general public of this very amusing collection. One of Thackeray's habits, from his schoolboy days, was to ornament the margins and blank pages of the books he had in use with caricature illustrations of their contents. This gave special value to the sale of his library, and is almost cause for regret that it could not have been preserved in its integrity. Thackeray's place in literature is eminent enough to have made this an interest to future generations. The anonymous editor has done the best that he could to compensate for the lack of this. He has obtained access to the principal works thus dispersed, and he speaks, not only of the readiness with which their possessors complied with his request, but of the abundance of the material spontaneously proffered to him. He has thus been able to reproduce in facsimile the five or six hundred sketches of this volume. They differ, of course, not only in cleverness, but in finish; but they unquestionably establish Thackeray's capability of becoming, if not an eminent artist, yet a great caricaturist. A grotesque fancy, an artistic touch, and a power of reproducing unmistakable portraits in comic exaggerations, as well as of embodying ludicrous ideas pictorially, make the book very amusing. Still more valuable is the descriptive, biographical, and anecdotal letterpress, which gives us a great accumulation of biographical information concerning Thackeray's works, reading, history, and habits. Without being a formal biography, it tells us scores of things that could scarcely have come into any biography. We have no clue to the sources of information possessed by the editor. Apparently he has been a most diligent student of his hero, and an indefatigable collector of scraps of information concerning his entire literary career. We can testify only to the great interest of the book, and to the vast amount of curious information which it contains. We regret that it has been published without the sanction of his family, but no admirer of Thackeray should be without it. It is an admirable addendum, not only to his collected works, but also to any memoir of him that has been, or that is likely to be written.*"—BRITISH QUARTERLY REVIEW.

Crown 8vo, cloth extra, gilt edges, with Illustrations, 7s. 6d.

Thomson's Seasons and Castle of Indolence.
With a Biographical and Critical Introduction by ALLAN CUNNINGHAM, and over 50 fine Illustrations on Steel and Wood.

Crown 4to, cloth extra, gilt and gilt edges, with Illustrations, 21s.

Thornbury's Historical and Legendary Ballads and Songs.
Illustrated by J. WHISTLER, JOHN TENNIEL, A. F. SANDYS, W. SMALL, M. J. LAWLESS, J. D. WATSON, G. J. PINWELL, F. WALKER, and others.

"*Mr. Thornbury has perceived with laudable clearness that one great requisite of poetry is that it should amuse. He rivals Goethe in the variety and startling incidents of his ballad-romances; he is full of vivacity and spirit, and his least impassioned pieces ring with a good out-of-doors music of sword and shield. Some of his mediæval poems are particularly rich in colour and tone. The old Norse ballads, too, are worthy of great praise. Best of all, however, we like his Cavalier songs; there is nothing of the kind in English more spirited, masculine, and merry.*"—ACADEMY.

"*Will be welcomed by all true lovers of art. . . . We must be grateful that so many works of a school distinguished for its originality should be collected into a single volume.*"—SATURDAY REVIEW.

Crown 8vo, cloth extra, 10s. 6d.

Cyril Tourneur's Collected Works,
including a unique Poem, entitled "The Transformed Metamorphosis;" and "Laugh and Lie Down; or, the World's Folly." Now first Collected, and Edited, with Critical Preface, Introductions, and Notes, by J. CHURTON COLLINS. [*In the press.*

Crown 8vo, cloth extra, with Illustrations, 7s. 6d.

J. M. W. Turner's Life and Correspondence.
Founded upon Letters and Papers furnished by his Friends and fellow Academicians. By WALTER THORNBURY. A New Edition, entirely rewritten and considerably en.¹ rged. With numerous Illustrations.

Crown 8vo, cloth extra, with Illustrations, 7s. 6d.

Timbs' Clubs and Club Life in London.
With Anecdotes of its famous Coffee-houses, Hostelries, and Taverns. By JOHN TIMBS, F.S.A. With numerous Illustrations.

"*The book supplies a much-felt want. The club is the avenue to general society of the present day, and Mr. Timbs gives the entrée to the club. The scholar and antiquary will also find the work a repertory of information on many disputed points of literary interest, and especially respecting various well-known anecdotes, the value of which only increases with the lapse of time.*"—MORNING POST.

Crown 8vo, cloth extra, with Illustrations, 7s. 6d.

Timbs' English Eccentrics and Eccentricities:
Stories of Wealth and Fashion, Delusions, Impostures, and Fanatic Missions, Strange Sights and Sporting Scenes, Eccentric Artists, Theatrical Folks, Men of Letters, &c. By JOHN TIMBS, F.S.A. With nearly 50 Illustrations.

"*The reader who would fain enjoy a harmless laugh in some very odd company might do much worse than take an occasional dip into 'English Eccentrics.' The illustrations are admirably suited to the letterpress.*"—GRAPHIC.

Crown 4to, half-Roxburghe, 12s. 6d.

Vagabondiana;
or, Anecdotes of Mendicant Wanderers through the Streets of London; with Portraits of the most Remarkable, drawn from the Life by JOHN THOMAS SMITH, late Keeper of the Prints in the British Museum. With Introduction by FRANCIS DOUCE, and Descriptive Text. With the Woodcuts and the 32 Plates, from the original Coppers.

Large crown 8vo, cloth antique, with Illustrations, 7s. 6d.

Walton and Cotton's Complete Angler;
Or, The Contemplative Man's Recreation: being a Discourse of Rivers, Fish-ponds, Fish and Fishing, written by IZAAK WALTON; and Instructions how to Angle for a Trout or Grayling in a clear Stream, by CHARLES COTTON. With Original Memoirs and Notes by Sir HARRIS NICOLAS, K.C.M.G. With the 61 Plate Illustrations, precisely as in Pickering's two-volume Edition.

"*Among the reprints of the year, few will be more welcome than this edition of the 'Complete Angler,' with Sir Harris Nicolas's Memoirs and Notes, and Stothard and Inskipp's illustrations.*"—SATURDAY REVIEW.

Crown 8vo, cloth extra, with Vignette Portrait, 9s.

Wells' Joseph and his Brethren:
A Dramatic Poem. By CHARLES WELLS. With an Introductory Essay by ALGERNON CHARLES SWINBURNE.

"*The author of 'Joseph and his Brethren' will some day have to be acknowledged among the memorable men of the second great period in our poetry. . . . There are lines even in the overture of his poem which might, it seems to me, more naturally be mistaken even by an expert in verse for the work of the young Shakspeare, than any to be gathered elsewhere in the fields of English poetry.*"—SWINBURNE.

"*In its combination of strength and delicacy, in sweet liquid musical flow, in just cadence, and in dramatic incisiveness of utterance, the language throughout keeps closer to the level of the Elizabethan dramatists than that of any dramatist of subsequent times.*"—ATHENÆUM.

Carefully printed on paper to imitate the Original, 22 in. by 14 in., price 5s.

The Warrant to Execute Charles I.
An exact Facsimile of this important Document, with the Fifty-nine Signatures of the Regicides, and corresponding Seals.

Beautifully printed on paper to imitate the Original MS., price 2s.

Warrant to Execute Mary Q. of Scots.

An exact Facsimile, including the Signature of Queen Elizabeth, and a Facsimile of the Great Seal.

In portfolios, price £4 4s. each series.

Wild's Cathedrals.

Select Examples of the Ecclesiastical Architecture of the Middle Ages; arranged in Two Series (the First FOREIGN, the Second ENGLISH). Each Series containing Twelve fine Plates, mounted upon Cardboard, and carefully Coloured, after the Original Drawings, by CHARLES WILD.

Three Vols. 8vo, with 103 Plates, exhibiting nearly four hundred figures of Birds, accurately engraved and beautifully printed in Colours, cloth extra, gilt, £3 3s.

Wilson's American Ornithology;

or, Natural History of the Birds of the United States; with the Continuation by Prince CHARLES LUCIAN BONAPARTE. New and Enlarged Edition, completed by the insertion of above One Hundred Birds omitted in the Original Work, and Illustrated by valuable Notes, and a Life of the Author, by Sir WILLIAM JARDINE.

"*The History of American Birds, by Alexander Wilson, is equal in elegance to the most distinguished of our own splendid works on Ornithology.*"—CUVIER.

*** Also a few Large Paper copies, 4to, with the Plates all carefully Coloured by hand, at £6 6s.

Crown 8vo, cloth extra, with Illustrations, 7s. 6d.

Wright's Caricature History of the

Georges. *(The House of Hanover.)* With 400 Pictures, Caricatures, Squibs, Broadsides, Window Pictures, &c. By THOMAS WRIGHT, Esq., M.A., F.S.A.

"*Emphatically one of the liveliest of books, as also one of the most interesting. Has the twofold merit of being at once amusing and edifying.*"—MORNING POST.

Large post 8vo, cloth extra, gilt, with Illustrations, 7s. 6d.

Wright's History of Caricature and of

the Grotesque in Art, Literature, Sculpture, and Painting, from the Earliest Times to the Present Day. By THOMAS WRIGHT, M.A., F.S.A. Profusely illustrated by F. W. FAIRHOLT, F.S.A.

"*A very amusing and instructive volume.*"—SATURDAY REVIEW.

www.ingramcontent.com/pod-product-compliance
Lightning Source LLC
Chambersburg PA
CBHW022111160426
43197CB00009B/977